Jet
Safari
to Africa

Jet
Safari
to Africa

Robert P. L. Straughan

SOUTH BRUNSWICK AND NEW YORK: A. S. BARNES AND COMPANY
LONDON: THOMAS YOSELOFF LTD

© 1973 by A. S. Barnes and Co., Inc.
Library of Congress Catalogue Card Number: 78-151126

A. S. Barnes and Co., Inc.
Cranbury, New Jersey 08512

Thomas Yoseloff Ltd
108 New Bond Street
London W1Y OQX, England

ISBN 0-498-07921-X
Printed in the United States of America

Contents

Preface

Each year more people seek out new areas of the world to visit. The modern jet plane has made the far corners of the earth no more than a day or two away. The adventurer—and the tourist who desires something different—is now turning to Africa, the stronghold of wild animals, the safari, the veldt. Here we have a giant continent so vast that one may travel 12 hours at jet speed and still not cover the whole land area. We have a continent that is different in every way from our own, and there is a surprise at every landing.

The trees are different, the birds are all unfamiliar, the natives speak a strange tongue. You expect hot weather on the equator and find that a sweater is needed almost until noon. You think you will be fighting insects and flies, but find your insect repellent practically unnecessary. Will the people be hostile? Is there personal danger to you? The people are warm and friendly, and you will find far less crime in darkest Africa than in your own home town. Here is a land of intrigue—a different kind of place to go. On safari you will sleep in a tent at the foot of Mt. Kilimanjaro, ride on the veldt, and drive right up to lion, elephant, and giraffe. Some will be so close you can almost reach out and touch them. Yet you will be far safer here than you would driving on the expressway during rush hour in any American city.

This book brings you a capsule glimpse of Africa, from Dakar, West Africa, to South Africa, Rhodesia, Zambia, Tanzania, and Kenya, covering a total distance of 23,000 miles—much of it by jet plane and the rest by landrover and minibus. A day-by-day, hour-by-hour description of the safari is presented in detail, most of it written as the events occurred. This is Africa as it is today.

Jet
Safari
to Africa

1. Africa, a Far Away Dream

I had always wanted to go to Africa, ever since I was four years old—the age I first learned about animals. I learned that all the really *big* animals—the elephant, the rhino, the hippo, the giraffe, the lion—came from the dark continent. I lived animals as a child, and when I first learned about libraries I borrowed and read every book about animals, particularly those from Africa.

I always planned to explore the jungles as far back as I can remember, but somehow I could never quite get to do it. I kept putting it off as something I would do *some day*. I became an undersea explorer and spent nearly 20 years swimming in the twilight zone of the mysterious undersea world. I was a true explorer with adventure! I was attacked by sharks and nearly stung to death by a deadly jellyfish; I found a real sunken galleon and almost became a millionaire. I explored the bottom of the sea, usually all alone, as I wished I could have explored the jungles of Africa. I spent a total of over 25,000 hours in the sea, which is about as much as any man alive today, and I made a good living at it. Even though my adventures were hair-raising (I faced almost certain death many times), I loved almost every minute of it. I wrote several books and hundreds of articles, many of which were featured in the *Saturday Evening Post, National Geographic,* and other magazines. I gave lectures and showed movies, and in between times spent my work days under the sea. I published my own magazine about marine life and it was very successful.

But one day I suddenly decided that I had enough of the sea. I began to think about Africa—the jungles, the veldt, the wild animals, the rain forests—and suddenly the thought of going there seemed within my grasp. It didn't seem as impossible as it had in the past. I had the money and the time, for I worked for myself and could take off any time I desired. There was really no reason at all why I shouldn't go. But then I began to put off the idea again. Was it just a vague dream?

I had read almost every book about Africa and had most of them in my home library. I knew by heart the areas that held the greatest concentrations of animals and which I would most like to visit. But I felt that I was not a free man who could just take off at the drop of a hat. I have a wife and two children, Paul who is twelve and Julie who is ten. I also have my own store where I sell colorful salt water fish, books, and marine aquarium equipment. I open the store only by appointment so that when I am closed, no one will come. Closing the store for a month would not be catastrophic. I had developed my business into largely mail-order so that the store was not my sole source of income. It seemed as though I was trying to invent reasons why I couldn't go to Africa. My family, particularly my wife, Rosemary, wanted me to go because I talked about it day and night.

Then one day, a great event happened in the world, one in which I had been keenly interested. MAN LANDED ON THE MOON! I watched the whole thing on television from start to finish with Paul, who was equally interested in the space effort. Then when I saw man actually step foot on the moon, I announced to my family that if the astronauts could go all the way to the moon and back, then I could surely go to Africa. Right then I made up my mind that I would go, not next year or the year after, but THIS year!

I decided to move fast, and my first stop was the local travel agency, Holiday Hunters at Dadeland Mall in Kendall. A charming and attractive lady named Joanne Paulk assisted me. I told her I wanted to go to Africa to see the jungles and the animals and she gave me a huge cluster of safari pamphlets that presented trips by different routes and different airlines. I brought them home and looked them over very carefully. Since I had read so many books on Africa, the names in the brochures were familiar to me: Treetops, Masai Mara, Ngorongoro, Serengeti. I evaluated the various itineraries and then finally settled down with a large, colorful, well-illustrated brochure from Pan American Airways and Percival Tours. The tours all looked so interesting I didn't know which one to choose.

Percival Tour No. 14, "African Highlights," offered the most of any tour, for it covered practically the entire continent. Besides including East Africa, it went to West Africa, then all the way to South Africa, then to Rhodesia, Zambia, and Victoria Falls. As I read the itinerary, I could hardly believe my eyes! The trip left from Kennedy Airport in New York. We would fly all the way by Pan American, non-stop, to Dakar in Senegal, West Africa. We would stay there a few days and then fly to Johannesburg in South Africa, then go to Kruger Park, then on to Rhodesia. Next would be Zambia and Victoria Falls. From there we would visit Nairobi in Kenya and Tanzania to see all the major game preserves in both countries. I was flabbergasted at the tremendous coverage of the trip.

At this point, however, I was still undecided whether I should take a guided tour or go to Africa by myself and catch a safari out of Nairobi. The trip by myself held promise of adventure, but then a trip of this magnitude by guided tour offered a lot in its favor. All the red tape, visas, permits, guides, luggage, hotel reservations, and both air and ground transportation would be handled for me by experts in the field so that I wouldn't have to bother with any of it. This appealed to me for I knew that a great deal of time could be wasted on the trip itself if I had to make arrangements for everything as I went along. I called up my good friend Paul Zahl of *National Geographic* and asked his opinion. Dr. Zahl has traveled around the world many times working on his fabulous articles for the magazine, and I felt certain he could advise me on the best procedure. I told him of my proposed journey and he suggested the guided tour as the most practical, especially since I would be traveling alone. That settled the matter. I would go on a guided tour with a group instead of by myself. It sounded like the most sensible plan.

My next step was another trip to the travel agency to find out more about the trip and its actual cost. Also I had to know whether or not there was time for me to get on the tour, as many are usually booked as much as a year ahead. I talked to Mrs. Paulk again and she assured me that I could get on the tour but that I would have to hurry as there was a great deal of work to be done on such short notice. When I told her I didn't even have a passport she said that I should start on that right away. She gave me full instructions on how and where to obtain it. I would also need two vaccinations—one for smallpox and one for yellow fever. She cautioned me that time slips by fast and that there was a great deal of paper work that had to be done. There would be many visas, reservations and confirmations for both travel and lodgings, and forms to fill out. In addition, since I would be traveling alone I would need single room supplement, which is much more difficult than sharing a room with a companion. I gave her a $150 deposit, which is required, so she could get down to the actual booking of the trip. She was very nice and most helpful.

I checked with her later on in the week to see if everything was all right and if I would be able to get on the tour. She announced that since I was traveling by myself she could not get me reservations for the scheduled departure date of my planned trip. I would have to leave *two weeks earlier* if I wanted to go this year. Now time *was* running out. I went down immediately for a smallpox vaccination from a local doctor that same afternoon.

The next day I went downtown in Miami to get my passport. This was a little more complicated than I had anticipated. First of all, you have to have special photographs taken for your passport, which have to be a special size on a certain type of paper. There was a passport photo studio close by so I had my photo taken there. I bought a dozen prints which cost about $6.00 and then I went up for my passport—which I didn't get. It seemed that although I had a stamped and certified copy of a card from my birth certificate office showing that my birth certificate was on file, it was not good enough. I had to have a copy of the actual document. The clerks in the passport office were curt, even rude. One shoved a sheet of paper in my hand and said that on the back of it I would find the address to which I could write for a copy of my birth certificate. He seemed very reluctant to tell me anything. When I asked him the address of his office so that I would know which department to mail the certificate to, instead of replying he sourly reached into his desk and took out a rubber stamp, stamping out an address on a piece of paper. What a pity I thought that the state department doesn't send around officials from time to time to check on their employees and see how they conduct themselves with the public.

Next, I went down for my yellow fever shot. Again, this is not as simple as it sounds, and can also be very complicated. First of all, you can only get the shot at a special office in the Federal Building. Your family doctor or a hospital cannot give it to you. Then, you can only get it on a certain day of the week and at a certain hour of the day. I just happened to hit it lucky for I accidentally went down on the day they were giving the shots. But I was *really* lucky, for I found out that if I had not gone down that day, I would have had to wait 30 days before I would be allowed to take the yellow fever shot. You must get this injection within 24 hours after you get the smallpox shot or you will have to wait 30 days before you can take it. It has something to do with the fact that both shots are live serums or something like that. At any rate, the doctor who gave me the smallpox shot should have told me that. If I hadn't gone for my shot and passport that precise day, my trip would have been off for another year, perhaps forever.

After getting the shot, I went to the post office to send an air mail letter for my birth certificate. To expedite the return of the document I enclosed the required one dollar and a self-addressed return envelope. There had been no charge for the yellow fever shot, which was quick and entirely painless. I did pay $10 for the smallpox shot, which I found out later I could have gotten for nothing. In addition, I had to take the vaccination card to the public health office to have it validated. I could have received the shot right there and saved both time and money.

While I was downtown I bought a leather flight bag supposedly small enough to fit under the seat of the plane so that I could carry it right along on the flights. It had a large zipper pocket on one side and two of them on the other. The center section opened up with a single zipper that went all around the bag. I figured I could keep my unexposed film and some of my equipment in the large pockets. (I found out later that it would not fit under the seat on *any* airplane, but it was a fine bag and was most useful.)

It had been an interesting day and I went home to relate the events to my family, who at this point had become excited as I about the trip. Then I tried to settle down into the normal routine of business, but it was not easy for I had set into motion a chain of events that could ultimately change my life. I wasn't just going on a simple trip. I would be fulfilling a life-long dream and ambition. Who knows what it would hold for the future? I found it difficult to concentrate on my daily business. In the not too distant future a great adventure awaited me.

Time flew! Departure date for the trip was two months away when I had first visited the travel agency. Because I did not want to double up with a total stranger, I was booked on the earlier trip. Departure date was now just one month away and I still didn't have my passport—or even my birth certificate! I filled out a great many forms at the travel agency for all the countries that we were to visit. Mrs. Paulk read me a letter from the tour headquarters in New York outlining the itinerary for the safari. The letter stated

that their office must have my passport within a few days so that they could obtain all the necessary visas for the long journey.

I checked my mail morning and night until the birth certificate arrived, and I promptly mailed it to the passport office in Miami asking them to please rush. I was getting a little worried at this point. Then just a couple of days later my passport arrived! I promptly brought it to the travel agency and Mrs. Paulk mailed it special delivery to the tour headquarters in New York. (It was several days past the deadline set by the tour office in their letter.) She gave me a handsome shoulder-type flight bag from Percival Tours that I could carry with me on the plane.

D-Day (departure day) was now approaching and I began to take the trip very seriously. I still couldn't convince myself that I was actually going and wouldn't believe it until I was on the plane headed for Africa.

I was told I would need several wash-and-dry shirts and slacks. Mrs. Paulk had given me a list of the various items recommended for the trip. We were limited to 44 pounds, which was to include everything we would need for a total of three weeks. I began the impossible task of packing clothes, shoes, a sweater, a raincoat, toilet utensils, flashlights, three cameras (two for stills and one for movies), approximately 100 rolls of film, a large 12-inch telephoto lens, and a unipod all into one small suitcase and the small shoulder bag. I found that my toilet utensils, which included a bottle of aspirins, pills, and medications, weighed several pounds just by themselves. The two biggest and bulkiest items were my 300mm telephoto lens, which weighed nearly five pounds, and my dress shoes. I decided to wear the dress shoes and pack the large lens in the suitcase surrounding it with the clothes for protection. I packed and repacked both bags several times before I got everything to fit. My total gear consisted of the following:

1 medium-sized executive flight bag
1 small handbag with shoulder strap
1 Super 8 Bell & Howell movie camera
1 Minolta 35mm still camera with a 4″ lens
1 300mm Telephoto lens for the Minolta
1 Alpa 35mm Reflex camera with wide angle lens
1 Unipod for telephoto lens (I never used it)
30 Rolls of 8mm movie film
70 Rolls of 35mm color film—Kodachrome 11 and Hi-Speed Ektachrome (about half of each), 2 Kodacolor. All 36 ex.
1 exposure meter
2 small flashlights (1 medium, 1 very tiny)
1 raincoat

1 suit
6 washable shirts
3 washable slacks
6 pr. washable underwear
6 pr. washable socks
2 pr. shoes—one dress, the other nylon mesh loafers
1 pr. binoculars, small 7x35
2 pocket knives
1 heavy woolen sweater (an absolute necessity)
2 large writing pads, 5″ x 8″
12 medium plastic bags
1 assortment of toilet articles—aspirin, band aids, antiseptic solution, bath powder, toothpaste, razor, etc. (I forgot a toothbrush)

The suitcase was the small 22-inch long flight bag that I mentioned earlier. I was told that I could carry it on the plane with me so I packed my Alpa camera in it along with all of the items mentioned above. The film fit very nicely in the huge zipper pockets on both sides of it. I put my movie camera and some film in the small shoulder bag as well as a small amount of clothing, my writing pads, and other items that I might need aboard the flight. When everything was finally packed, I placed both bags on the family scale and the total weight was only 39 pounds—much to my surprise. I had purposely kept the weight down so that I would be able to carry souvenirs back with me and still not go over the weight limit. At this point I was becoming more and more excited about the trip, but I still wouldn't believe that I was really going until I was on the plane. The travel bureau handled all the complicated details and it looked like all systems were go for the trip.

Then just ten days before D-Day I came home and found an innocuous-looking letter from New Orleans lying on the table. At first I thought it was just another advertisement and almost tossed it away. Then I glanced at the return address and noticed the words, "Consulate Office." I picked up the letter and hesitatingly opened it wondering why I would be getting a letter from the Consulate Office. There were a number of forms and instructions enclosed with a letter from the South African Consulate. It said that they were very sorry but the old forms for visas to South Africa were no longer acceptable in that country and that I should fill out all the new forms posthaste and return them to their office. They said they had my passport in their office in good keeping. I filled out all the forms immediately and sent them back special delivery to New Orleans. This could cancel out my whole trip I thought!

It was now one week before departure. I stopped by the travel bureau to see if they wanted me to pay the balance of the bill for the safari. According to the terms on the brochure, the entire amount must be paid in full 30 days before departure, but still my local travel agency had not asked for the balance. I told Mrs. Paulk about my letter from New Orleans and that I was concerned whether or not these papers would hold up my trip. She said she thought I would still get all my papers in time. She suggested that I bring extra money for the trip in traveler's checks as well as some cash. Her fellow agent, Dee Burrus, suggested at least $100 in cash (most of it in one dollar bills) for buying little gifts or souvenirs all over Africa. I purchased $250 in traveler's checks, all $10 checks, and decided to bring $250 in cash, of which $60 was in one-dollar bills.

The big safari was now only a half a week away. Mrs. Paulk had called to tell me she had my passport. I stopped by her office to pick it up and she said she would write up my tickets for the trip the next day and I could then pay the balance. She apparently had been waiting for the visas for all the countries I would visit, but now that we had the passport all stamped and in hand, it looked as though the trip was completely confirmed.

I received a number of pamphlets from Percival Tours: a list of all the hotels in which we would stay on the trip and our mailing address for each, a currency converter explaining the money of the different countries, more instructions on what to take, and a temperature chart listing the high and low temperatures in the various countries. Then there was a final itinerary No. 14 that read as follows:

PERCIVAL TOURS INC.
Africa Highlights   Final Itinerary   No. 14   1969
Visiting Senegal, South Africa, Rhodesia, Zambia, Kenya, Tanzania

Monday, Sept. 22
New York. You are requested to be at the Pan American World Airways Check In Counter at New York Kennedy International Airport by 6:00 P.M.
Leave New York (Kennedy International Airport) at 7:10 P.M. via Pan American World Airways flight #PA/156, flying into:

SENEGAL
Tuesday, Sept. 23
Arrive Dakar (Yoff Airport) at 6:50 A.M. You will be met and transferred from the airport to the Grand Hotel De N'Gor.
Our afternoon city tour of Dakar includes visits to the main places of interest, such as the Kermel and Sandaga markets, the Cathedral, National Assembly, The Museum of History and Ethnography, Law Courts, and the Presi-

dential Palace. In the native markets, women in gaily colored costumes sell lace products and the Moors from the Northern deserts offer intricate silverwork for sale.

Wednesday, Sept. 24

Leave Dakar (Yoff Airport) by Pan American World Airways flight #PA/150 at 5:30 A.M. flying into:

SOUTH AFRICA

To arrive Johannesburg (Jan Smuts Airport) at 9:00 P.M. President Hotel

Thursday, Sept. 25

We leave Johannesburg this morning and drive over the grassy plains of the Highveld at 6000 feet, to Machadodorp, then down the escarpment to the pretty orange-growing districts of Nelspruit and White River in the Lowveld at 2000 feet. Entering Kruger Park at the Numbi Gate, we drive to the Pretorius Kop Rest Camp.

Friday, Sept. 26

In Kruger Park. This whole day is devoted to game viewing in the famous Kruger Park—well known for its lions—visiting hippo pools, and driving along the Sabie River Banks. Herds of animals come to drink at the river and sometimes elephant and buffalo may be seen. Wildebeeste, impala, waterbuck and many other species of game can usually be seen. Overnight camp at Skukuza Rest Camp.

Saturday, Sept. 27

After an early morning game drive, we leave Kruger Park and drive through Nelspruit, continuing up the escarpment road to the open grasslands of the Highveld, past gaily decorated villages of the Ndebele, a tribal offshoot of the Zulus, back to Johannesburg. President Hotel.

MEMBERS TAKING THE OPTIONAL 3-DAY EXCURSION TO CAPE TOWN WILL TRAVEL AS FOLLOWS:

Thursday, Sept. 25

Leave Johannesburg (Jan Smuts Airport) by South African Airways flight #SA/319 at 10:00 A.M. to arrive Cape Town (D. F. Malan Airport) at 11:55 A.M. Grand Hotel. In the afternoon, enjoy a tour of the city, a blend of the old and the new, driving through its narrow streets that recall Dutch Colonial days, and then through rows of tall office buildings, modern as tomorrow. Also visit the Michaelis Collection of Flemish and Dutch paintings, and the South African Museum with its famous African Room. Then by cableway, ascend to the top of Table Mountain from where you have a breathtaking panoramic view over the city, the Atlantic and Indian Oceans.

Friday, Sept. 26

In Cape Town. This day will be spent on a Grand Tour of the Cape Peninsula, driving first to the Rhodes Memorial and then through beautiful vineyards to the old Dutch Homesteads of Constantia. Via Muizenburg and St. James, arrive at the Cape of Good Hope, called by Sir Francis Drake: "The fairest Cape we saw in the whole circumference of the globe." The return journey is along the magnificent marine drive bordering the Atlantic Coast, past the towering crags of Chapman's Peak, Hout Bay and Sea Point.

Saturday, Sept. 27

In Cape Town. Morning at leisure for independent activities. Leave Cape Town (D. F. Malan Airport) by South African Airways flight #SA/316 at 6:30 P.M. to arrive Johannesburg (Jan Smuts Airport) at 8:10 P.M. President Hotel.

Sunday, Sept. 28

In Johannesburg. This morning we will enjoy the vividly colorful Native Mine Dances—the highlight of any Johannesburg visit. Contests are held between teams of different tribes, each with its own costumes and particular type of dancing, perhaps the most exciting of which is the War Dance of the Zulus, who shake the ground with their rhythmically stamping feet.

In the afternoon, we shall visit the city and its suburbs, driving through towering modern buildings to the rolling, tree-clad hills of the residential districts, with their many spacious parks.

Monday, Sept. 29

Leave Johannesburg (Jan Smuts Airport) by South African Airlines flight #SA/250 at 10:50 A.M. flying into:

RHODESIA

To arrive Bulawayo at 11:55 A.M. Change planes and leave Bulawayo by Air Rhodesia, flight #RH/812 at 1:40 P.M., to arrive Victoria Falls at 2:45 P.M.

Upon arrival, visit the Livingstone Monument and then proceed to visit the magnificent Victoria Falls—twice as high and one and a half times wide as Niagara—pouring 75 million gallons a minute over the Main Falls, all of which are visited, as well as the spray-soaked Rain Forests and the precipitous Knife Edge. Cross the border into:

ZAMBIA

to Livingstone. Inter-Continental Hotel.

Tuesday, Sept. 30

In Livingstone. This morning we visit the Livingstone National Museum, a scientific and cultural center of international repute, and a fascinating storehouse of the history, prehistory, culture and art of Zambia. It is also famous for its collection of Livingstone memorabilia. Continue for a tour of the city, the most historic in Zambia, stopping at the Tourist Center, the Barotse Gardens and the Curio Shop. There will be time for shopping.

This afternoon, we visit the Open Air Livingstone Museum, a cluster of tribal dwellings established to preserve the ancient arts and crafts. See the expert wood-carvers, Luvale blacksmiths fashioning hunting spears, and craftsmen carving Likishi masks. Proceed to Livingstone Game Park to see zebra, kudu and antelope and perhaps the rare white rhino, found nowhere else in Zambia.

This evening we will drive to the Eastern Cataract, to enjoy the spectacular sight of the floodlit Falls thundering into the Gorge below.

Wednesday, Oct. 1

In Livingstone. The morning is at leisure for shopping or independent activities.

In the cool of the early evening, we board the "Zambesi Queen" for a leisurely cruise up the Zambesi River, during which we may see hippos wallowing in the river, Goliath

Heron and an abundance of bird life, including the strange Lily Trotter, which lives on the water lilies floating in the river. We may also see crocodiles and elephant on the banks.

Thursday, Oct. 2

Leave Livingstone by Zambia Airlines flight #QZ/547 at 1:40 P.M., to arrive Lusaka at 2:30 P.M. Change planes and leave Lusaka by Zambia Airlines flight #QZ/510 at 3:10 P.M. flying into:

KENYA

to arrive Nairobi (Embakasi Airport) at 8:10 P.M. New Stanley Hotel.

Friday, Oct. 3

Leave Nairobi and drive via Thika and Chania Falls to Nyeri for lunch at the Outspan Hotel. Continue to the world-famous Treetops Hotel. Here 40 feet above the ground, the night is spent watching elephant, rhino, buffalo, and small game as they come to drink at the water hole beneath the hotel's observation deck.

Saturday, Oct. 4

Leave Treetops this morning and return to Nyeri for breakfast at the Outspan Hotel, after which a short drive takes us across the Equator to Nanyuki and the luxurious Mt. Kenya Safari Club—fabulous millionaire's resort on the slopes of Mt. Kenya. The balance of the day is at leisure to enjoy the fine facilities of the club—part owned by movie star William Holden—including swimming, tennis and horseback riding.

Sunday, Oct. 5

Leave Nanyuki this morning and drive via the Great Rift Valley back to Nairobi. New Stanley Hotel.

Monday, Oct. 6

In Nairobi. A morning city tour of Nairobi includes a visit to the National Museum with its exhibits of Dr. Leaky's discoveries of pre-historic man in Kenya, and the Aviary. Continue to the Arboretum, Government buildings, the university and the residential areas.

This afternoon we shall leave Nairobi, driving south across the wide Athi Plains—home of the proud Masai people—to the famous Amboseli Game Preserve. Amboseli Camp.

In the afternoon, the road leads through the reserve, home of Black Rhino, where many types of large and small game may be seen in their primeval surroundings, while over all looms the majestic, snow-capped dome of Mt. Kilimanjaro, Africa's highest mountain (19,340 feet).

Tuesday, Oct. 7

After an early morning game drive, we leave Amboseli and drive across the border into:

TANZANIA

continuing via Arusha—situated beneath 15,000 ft. Mt. Meru and located precisely half way between the Cape and Cairo—continuing our drive westward to Ngorongoro Lodge, built on the crater's rim.

Wednesday, Oct. 8

In Ngorongoro. Land Rovers will take us down 2,000 feet to the 100-square-mile crater floor of Ngorongoro for a full day of game viewing in this wonderland of wild animals, where vast herds of game graze and where lion, elephant, rhino and hippo as well as a variety of birds may be seen.

Thursday, Oct. 9

This morning we leave Ngorongoro and drive via the Olduvai Gorge, where traces of pre-historic man and animals have been found, and continue across the famous Serengeti Plains in Serengeti National Park—center of the largest concentration of game in the world—to arrive at Seronera Safari Camp in time for lunch.

This afternoon will be devoted to game-viewing in Serengeti, famous for its numerous lions and for the countless number of other animals which abound in the region.

Friday, Oct. 10

After breakfast at the lodge, we enjoy another morning of game viewing in this famous reserve. Leaving Serengeti in the afternoon, we drive northwards through the Park and cross into:

KENYA

continuing to the Masai-Mara Game Reserve, for a two nights stay at the Keekorok Lodge or Tented Camp.

Saturday, Oct. 11

In Masai-Mara Game Reserve. Morning and afternoon game drives into the Reserve with its large prides of lions, elephant, buffalo and giraffe.

Sunday, Oct. 12

We leave Masai-Mara Game Reserve this morning, driving up the escarpment, to arrive Nairobi in time for lunch. New Stanley Hotel.

Monday, Oct. 13

Leave Nairobi (Embakasi Airport) by Alitalia Airlines flight #AZ/817 at 1:00 A.M. flying into:

ITALY

to arrive Rome at 5:50 A.M. Change planes and leave Rome by Pan American World Airways flight #PA/111 at 11:00 A.M. flying into the:

UNITED STATES OF AMERICA

to arrive New York (Kennedy International Airport) at 3:20 P.M.

This was how the itinerary read. In the following chapters I will give you a day-by-day, hour-by-hour description of the tour as it actually happened, how closely it adhered to the itinerary, and whether or not myself and others were pleased with it.

Departure time was now just a few days away. Mrs. Paulk had given me a final figure on the land and air costs of the trip (which was close to the brochure figure). The total cost was $1,950.00 which included my round trip fare to New York. This of course included all plane fares, hotels, meals, and ground transportation for the entire trip—everything! She wished me a pleasant voyage and I told her I would drop her a card. Then, with tickets in hand, I was on my way. It looked like I had finally made it. My family of course was excited, and I told the children I would try to telephone them from Livingstone if it was possible. I had checked with the long-distance operator and she said it would cost about $12.00 for a three-minute call from Rhodesia. I didn't think that was much considering the enormous distance. I had repacked my bags, slightly adding a few last-minute items, and began closing down my store and tending to last-minute details.

It was now two days before actual flight time. I began to think about my trip with increasing apprehension. To me, going all the way to Africa, to all the many countries we would visit, seemed almost like an impossible voyage. I seriously wondered whether I would make it back alive. Mrs. Paulk had told me that I would have to sleep in a tent in one of the game preserves, as there wasn't room in the main lodge for a single accommodation. This somewhat worried me. Imagine, sleeping in a tent by myself in the wilds of Africa! What if an elephant or a lion decided to crash through, or a hostile native invaded the tent in the dark of night. I couldn't bring a weapon, but at least I would have my flashlight and my pocket knife, I mused. Maybe I wouldn't sleep at all if the situation looked too precarious.

One day to go. The travel folder said to bring two suits but I was determined to bring only one. However, it did say to bring a wrinkle-proof suit, and mine wasn't, so I bought a new one at the last minute. My Alpa camera broke down and I had to send it air mail special delivery to New York to get it repaired in time for the trip. I had bought a new camera besides (the Minolta) and also about $300 worth of film. I was told it is better to buy the film here than to buy it abroad as it would be both fresher and less expensive. I had brought more camera equipment than most tourists would normally bring as I felt I would be able to take enough photos for a possible book on the trip. Also I was trying to start a new animal magazine and wanted to take as many photographs as possible for background material.

I spent my last day around the house so I could be with my family. I would miss them of course. Paul wanted me to bring him a large Hippo tooth; Julie wanted a native doll, a rare sea shell, or some native handicraft; my wife wanted anything so long as it didn't take up much room. Ellis Skolfield wanted a "real old" camel saddle; Bob Austin wanted some baby crowned Cranes; Fred Leonard wanted some blue stone from Tanzania; and the postman wanted some African stamps. The children also wanted African money, particularly coins, from as many countries as I could get them. Time went by a little slower on that

last day. I didn't want to exert myself, so I could rest up for the long journey ahead.

Departure time is now less than 20 hours away. I am becoming more and more excited. Then disaster struck! All of a sudden I developed a horrible, howling toothache that felt like the whole top of my head would fall off. What a time to get a toothache. It was Sunday afternoon and all the dentists were closed. What should I do? Surely I can't go all the way to Africa with a toothache. I tried to reach my dentist, Dr. Robert Leeds, who wasn't around. Finally his wife called and said she would have him call me. Hours went by and in desperation my wife called some emergency number and we got hold of a dentist who said he could see me in an hour. I rushed over to his office where he examined my teeth and took X-rays. I thought that perhaps I had busted a filling but it turned out much worse than that. He said that I had an abscess under my tooth and that in view of my impending trip I should have it operated on—that very night. He said that he couldn't do the work there as it was rather complicated. By now, the tooth had stopped aching (which is usually the case at the dentist's). The dentist gave me the X-rays to take along in case I decided to seek dental help on my trip. I thanked him and drove home, quite weary after the ordeal. Things didn't look good on the eve before Africa.

When I got home, my old friend Dr. Leeds called to inquire about my tooth and also why I hadn't been to see him in four years. I told him I thought I was only supposed to see my dentist every ten years (joking of course). He asked me about my tooth and I told him of my predicament and my intended journey to Africa tomorrow. Then he offered to see me the first thing in the morning, which I thought was very nice since I had not been to see him for so long. He said that perhaps he could give me a prescription for strong pain killers to take with me but that he would like to look at the tooth. At this point, I wasn't even sure whether I would have time to make it to the dentist office before my departure. My tooth quit aching though and soon I was fast asleep.

I woke up in fair spirits, although the thought of leaving my loved ones made me sad. I ate breakfast, took one gulp of hot coffee, and presto, my tooth woke up with a painful howl. I decided I should go to see Dr. Leeds, who kindly squeezed me in for a 9:30 appointment. When I got there, he looked over the situation and decided that since I was leaving for my trip that morning, perhaps we should take a chance and leave it alone, as there wouldn't be time to operate. He felt that the abscess would probably quiet down.

I had a head cold and he said this was causing it to act up more than usual. He gave me prescriptions for two drugs, one regular pain killer and an extra strong one to be taken as a last resort should the pain become unbearable. He wished me a happy voyage and set up an appointment for me upon my return.

Then I went home and spent a few pleasant moments with my wife. I had already said goodbye to Paul and Julie and I knew I would miss them. It was now time to leave so Rosemary and I drove to the airport. I said a quick goodbye and I was off to Africa on the first leg of my journey!

2.   Off at Last—Dakar, Senegal

Monday, Sept. 22

I left Miami by Eastern Airlines at noon. I arrived at the airport sooner than expected and took an earlier plane rather than hang around. The travel agency had stressed getting to New York in plenty of time so that in case of a delay in landing, due to flight stacking, I wouldn't miss my evening departure flight on Pan American. The plane took off from Miami about 15 minutes after I got aboard.

We had lunch aboard (including free champagne) and I was careful not to chew on the side of the abscess. The pain had largely subsided so I asked for milk instead of coffee. I didn't want to take any chances. We had a fine flight at 29,000 feet—high above the clouds. I took movies of the plane just before we took off and also of the flight itself, showing the beautiful clouds framed below the huge wings. It was a quick trip and before I knew it we were already landing in New York. I made a short movie of the smooth landing for my movie sequence and chalked up one flight of the many I would be making in the next few weeks. I picked up my suitcase at the baggage ramp. I now had a four-hour wait for the Pan Am flight to Dakar.

I had plenty of time so I decided to walk over to the Pan American building from the Eastern Terminal. It was only about a thousand feet away, but with my two bags the walk was extremely tiring. Mrs. Paulk at the travel agency had told me that Pan American would send a car for me if I requested it but it looked so near I decided to walk rather than wait for a car. I finally made it to the entrance of the huge, modern

Pan American terminal and checked in my heavy suitcase to Dakar. I had to show my passport for the first time. I watched my suitcase disappear down the baggage ramp and wondered if I would ever see it again. If it got lost, I would have no clothes or film for the trip. Almost everything I brought with me was in that bag. I hoped that the large zipper on my heavy suitcase would hold. Then I decided not to worry about it and sat in the terminal waiting for the 7:45 P.M. departure. It was an interesting place and I saw people from all over the world coming and going. There was a strange murmur clearly audible in the building that was caused from thousands of voices all reflecting from the ceiling. I went over to the customs agent and gave him a list of my cameras, which he stamped for me. I was told this was a wise procedure so that when I came back into the country I could show the slip, should there be any question as to whether or not I had purchased the equipment abroad. There was a beautiful restaurant upstairs, overlooking the vast airport, but I didn't eat anything as I knew we would be wined and dined on the next flight.

An announcement over the loudspeaker requested that all passengers going on Percival Tour No. 14 should report to the departure gate. I hurried over and was met by a Press Photographer from Pan American or Percival. He requested that we all stand together in a group to have our photo taken. Some of the group didn't want to get in the picture but those who agreed held a banner for Percival Tours. I was briefly introduced to some of the people on the tour at that time. Then I went back to my seat and waited for the departure. There were so many people in the terminal that I couldn't tell which ones were going on the tour except for an occasional glimpse of a Percival flight bag, which identified tour members. I didn't notice any young people. Finally flight time was here and we boarded the plane. My African journey had begun!

We took off just after dark, and as we left the captain turned off all the cabin lights so we could see the lights from the city, which looked like a gigantic Christmas tree. Soon we were up and away. I sat with an elderly lady who was also going on the tour. She said that she had chosen the trip because of the tremendous coverage of Africa that it offered. She had traveled often and was convinced that taking a guided tour was the only way to go because everything is arranged for you. On the other side of me a man from Dallas, Texas, who was going to Ghana on business, asked about our tour and I let him read the itinerary. He thought it would be quite an interesting trip. He told us that on his last trip to Africa he had caught Malaria.

We flew at 33,000 feet and the trip was to take seven hours. Imagine just *seven hours* to fly all the way from New York to Africa! It sounded incredible. The flight was very smooth and from time to time I could look out the window and see, when there was an opening in the clouds, the cold Atlantic glimmering far below. We had a very fine dinner at about 9:00 P.M., after which malaria pills were given to everyone. We were to take two pills each week while we were in Africa and, as a precaution, two for the first week after we returned.

We flew to Africa by Pan American Jet Clipper, high above the Atlantic. (Courtesy Pan American World Airways)

After dinner it was announced that a movie would be shown and there would be a $2.50 charge to listen to it. On each seat there was a special plug where earphones could be plugged in for those who wished to hear the movie. I thought this was rather ridiculous to pay $2,000 for a plane trip and then be charged for a movie. I didn't want to hear it anyhow. I would rather listen to the strong, constant purr of the mighty jet engines. The movie program was a complete fiasco. The stewardess had difficulty in getting the projector to stay in place as it hung down from the ceiling. It would show half on and off the screen. Furthermore, those who were using the earphones complained that the sound was not synchronized with the picture and it was only coming out of one earphone instead of both. The projector in back of me fared even worse. I looked back to see yards and yards of movie film spewing out of the ceiling on to the floor. The stewardess had frantically summoned the Captain to help her and he was crunching together huge coils of film that were spreading about the cabin like a giant snake. He was jamming it into the hat rack over the seats. It was hysterical, far funnier than the movie itself. They finally had to shut off the projector and refund the money.

It was now rather late and the cabin lights were turned off so we could sleep. The seats on the plane were extremely narrow. They are all right for two or three hours in the air but for a long, overnight flight they are downright uncomfortable, particularly when three people must crowd into the narrow space. Sleep was most difficult but I did get a few catnaps. I would wake up from time to time and look out the window to see the huge, cold, black wings of the giant jet carrying us high above the Atlantic. I couldn't help but marvel at the Jet Age and the fact that man had built such a fabulous machine. I must have slept more than I thought for suddenly all of the lights in the cabin came on. We were approaching Africa. I was very excited, and as I looked outside the sun was rising—a beautiful sight. I glanced at my watch and it was just 2:30 A.M., then I thought of the time difference between the two continents. The stewardess gave us hot towels to help wake us up and to wash with briefly. A half hour later we were making our descent to Dakar, Senegal, on the extreme Western edge of Africa. We had a smooth landing just as a thunder storm hit and I made movies of the plane as it touched down. I had made it to Africa at last.

Tuesday, Sept. 23

We got out of the plane and walked toward the

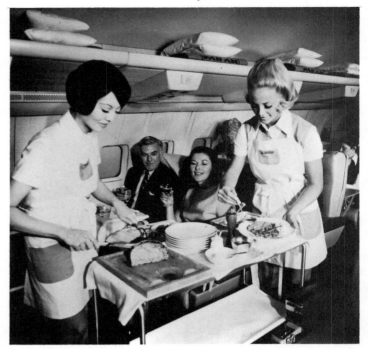

During a smooth flight at 33,000 feet, we were served a fine dinner. (Courtesy Pan American World Airways)

terminal. As I stopped to take a picture of the plane I found that my camera was completely fogged up, apparently from lying on the cold floor of the cabin during the long flight. I looked about the airport, already expecting to see wild animals. I saw some large, strange birds, some type of vulture or giant sea gull, flying about. Then we walked into the terminal and I could hear a native drum beating. I was thrilled to actually be in Africa.

Just inside the door of the terminal, our Percival Guide, Mr. Steven Charing, was there to meet and welcome us. He introduced himself and told us to call him Steve. We were told not to worry about our luggage and that as soon as he tended to our immigration and passport formalities we would be driven to our hotel. He asked that we all stay together as a group and get acquainted with each other while he attended to our baggage. After handling everything Steve took us aboard a waiting bus and after a short drive we arrived at the Grand Hotel. It was now about 7:00 A.M. African time, so we were just in time for breakfast. Everyone in the hotel spoke only French so it took a considerable dialogue between Steve and the waiters before our various orders of juice, eggs, toast, etc. could be translated. We were given canned orange juice and the coffee was extremely black and strong, almost like soup. We were all very tired and sleepy so no one ate much. Steve told us that there was no tipping and that all our food and drink was paid for, unless it was something that was not on the menu. We were expected to pay for soft drinks, bottled water, or alcoholic beverages ourselves as this was not included in the tour. We were served hot toast, eggs with bacon, fresh papaya, and more juice for those who requested it. After breakfast we were given our room numbers and some went immediately to their rooms to rest.

Our first stop was Dakar, Senegal, in West Africa, where we stayed at The Grand Hotel, one of the most beautiful in the entire country.

The hotel was very charming and the grounds were absolutely beautiful, with flower gardens and terraced lawn leading down to the sea. But it was also unusual, to say the least, and full of surprises. I had room 202, which I assumed would be on the second floor. I started walking up the stairs and soon found that they came to a dead end. Then I walked back downstairs and took another flight, which went up one floor and then came back down on the other side of the hotel. There were many stairways but they all ended at a private room. Finally, one of the natives who realized my plight came running to assist me. He insisted that 202 was not on the second floor but the *sixth*. He took me up in the elevator, then down a long, deserted hallway, and finally up a flight of stairs ending in another dark hallway. Taking out a huge key and turning it in the lock, he motioned me inside. I was a little hesitant, not knowing what to expect at this point, but I finally entered the room. The native followed me inside, opened all the windows, and showed me my luggage, which was mysteriously right there in the room, all intact. I had last

seen it disappearing down the ramp at Kennedy Airport. Then he motioned for me to follow him upstairs (my room had two floors, with stairways to the upper level) and showed me my bed and the toilet. He was a very friendly fellow with a huge, happy smile so I gave him a slight tip, which he seemed to appreciate immensely.

As soon as he left I set about to survey the situation. The room, built on two levels with a private balcony overlooking the sea, contained a couch, chairs, and bathroom on the lower level. A set of circular stairs led up to the bedroom and an additional private bath. Whoever built this hotel certainly must have liked stairs! The bed was interesting—round and tufted with a single pillow in the center. Hanging down from the ceiling was huge mosquito netting that completely encircled it.

Indeed, the whole place was strange. Not only was the hotel most unusual, but the natives, who wore dark robes and walked silently about the grounds, were equally so. They looked a little like ghouls—or like the grim reaper—as I watched them come and go from my balcony. I saw a brilliant, fire-red bird flying about the tree tops far below. I could look out to a spectacular ocean view and watch local fishermen cast their nets. I was pleased that Percival Tours had selected such a charming hotel as one of the stops for our trip.

It had been suggested that we get some sleep as we would have to rise at 3:30 the next morning for the next leg of our journey, but I was far too excited to sleep. How could you possibly sleep with all these strange and wonderful things about you? I decided to explore the area and do my sleeping on the plane if necessary. I took a quick bath, changed clothes, and took the elevator (the only way down) to the ground floor. I never found a stairway that went all the way down and quickly gave up on that.

The grounds about the hotel were breathtaking: beautiful green lawns were everywhere, with exotic flowers and shrubs set artistically along the edges. Perhaps a hundred or more natives were energetically working on the lawns and it looked like they were pulling out grass to thin them. Noticing a pathway leading out into a wild area that eventually terminated at the sea, I walked down to explore the shore, which was an interesting rocky area with large, black volcanic boulders strewn along it. I skipped among them, looking into the tide pools to see what kind of marine life the area might contain. To my astonishment, I saw hundreds of tiny jewel-like fish in no more than two or three inches of water, practically on the shore. They were almost exactly like the Caribbean Jewel fish (*Microspathodon chrysurus*), particularly the smaller, half-inch-long specimens. They were dark blue with light blue dots, spread evenly about the body, that glistened like so many jewels. The larger specimens looked like a cross between the Caribbean Beau Gregory and the Jewel Fish. The shape was like the Beau Gregory but the color was identical to the Jewel. The basic difference was that the fish had a large ocellus or "false eye" at the base of the dorsal. I am sure that the fish is not new to science, living so close to shore, but to the marine aquarium field, it undoubtedly is. Hence I named it the Peacock Jewel Fish, should it ever make its debut into the home aquarium market.

I was very excited about my find and after returning to the hotel for lunch, I inquired as to whether or not I could rent a face mask and swim fins so that I could explore the reefs around the area. I found a place that would rent me some and in less than five minutes I was diving on the strange reefs, where I saw many more of the little jewel fish and also numerous varieties of blennies and wrasses—all of which were quite new to me. I saw a butterfly fish that looked like a cross between the Pacific Chelmon Rostratus and the Atlantic Banded Butterfly. They were the same color as the Chelmon but they did not have the long nose. There were also spectacular spotted trigger fish, striped tangs, colorful wrasses, and many fish that I would expect to see in the Red Sea. The rocks and corals were covered with small anemones that produced a sharp sting when I brushed against them. I examined them closely for clownfish but saw none. There were hundreds of little blennies, an interesting little fish that skips about the rocks, and they were of many different species. It was so interesting to dive in a strange, new area.

A native boat along the strange, rocky coast at Dakar.

Our afternoon schedule called for a tour of the city so I finished my swim and got dressed for the tour. I was very anxious to see more of this unusual place. As we boarded a clean, *air-conditioned* bus (air-conditioned here means all windows opened) we were introduced to our local guide for the tour, a very attractive Dakar native named Hannah with sparkling white teeth. She pointed out things of interest to us as we drove around Dakar, a large, modern city of about 500,000 and the capital of Senegal. We would be taken on a 40-mile tour of the entire city. We had hardly left the hotel when I saw my first Baobab tree, a strange tree of huge dimensions that looks like it is growing upside down with its roots sticking into the air. It is also called the *monkey-bread* tree and is quite famous all throughout Africa. The trees grow to enormous dimensions, sometimes 20 or more feet in diameter, and its inside is often hollow. In some areas of Africa natives live inside the hollow tree, and even some native jails are made there. We came across numerous baobabs and one was of truly colossal size. It was in among a settlement of small homes and we didn't stop to investigate it as there were a great many natives about, who are very friendly but who are also super-salesmen. Every time our bus stopped they would immediately crowd about trying to sell us all kinds of little gifts, jewelry, and hand-carved items of native wood.

We stopped at a small village by the sea and I never saw such high-pressure salesmen in my life. If you showed the slightest interest in any object—a carved mask or a piece of native jewelry—they would try to sell it to you. They would start with a high price of 8,000 francs and would go all the way down to a thousand francs, even less, when you walked away. We were instructed by Steve ahead of time that in Africa you purchase things from the natives by bargaining, never accepting the first price they offer, which is always ridiculously high, as they expect you to bargain with them until you reach an agreeable price. It worked out exactly as he said and he would often come over to us and help us with the bargaining or offer his opinion as to whether or not a certain item was worth the price.

We saw the natives making the exquisite wood carvings right in their shops and we had an opportunity to buy authentic handiwork directly from them. I bought a little native doll for my daughter, Julie, with the same type of dress that our guide Hannah was wearing, and also a few other carved wood items. I didn't want to buy too much as it was at the beginning of our trip and I felt that I would have many opportunities to make purchases further on. (I did see many

A native marketplace beside the road in Dakar.

The women carried their babies papoose style here.

fine items here that I never saw in any other areas and had I known this I would have purchased more.)

We took a few photos of the natives in the shops but many were superstitious and reluctant to have their photos taken. Others wanted pay for having their pictures taken, which we later learned was expected in most areas of Africa. The town itself was very crowded with people, and it is a fact that the people have not heard of the population explosion or the pill. Most of the younger women carried a baby—papoose style—on their back. Natives were everywhere, walking along the highways or sleeping alongside the road. They would simply spread out a goat skin any place they wanted to lie down and go off to sleep—a most practical idea.

We traveled completely around the modern city in a large circle and noted its many beautiful buildings, including the university with its lavish grounds and ultra-modern architecture. We also went by the Palace of the President. While we stopped to photograph the building, our bus driver got out of the bus and spread a small carpet on the ground. Then he said his prayers leaning over and putting his head to the ground in the Moslem tradition. (Many of the people in the area are Moslems.) We visited a beautiful Mosque where we had to take off our shoes before entering it. Outside there were children begging for money and the usual salesmen trying to sell us their goods. We visited a native food market, but the flies were so heavy it was not the choicest of spots. I didn't even get out of the bus. We were all getting thirsty at this point so we stopped at the Brassière Snack Shop for a cold drink. Most of us had Coca-Cola, which we found available all over the continent. Then we stopped to photograph the Island of Goree, a small island about a half mile from shore where millions of slaves were

Here is one of the many ultra-modern buildings in the city.

The colorful guards at the palace are something to see.

held and shipped to the United States. The slave houses and many of the original buildings have been preserved there and it is a popular tourist attraction. I would like to have visited it but we didn't have time. I would also like to have visited Joal, an island of sea shells 74 miles from Dakar.

We returned to the hotel in time for evening meals and fortunately Trudy Kemeny sat at our table. She was traveling on the tour with us and she spoke nine languages. We were at a total loss as to what to order for dinner from the French menu and the waiters didn't understand a single word of English. Mrs. Kemeny easily translated the items for us and then translated them to the waiter with equal aplomb. I had a delicious local-fish dinner with potatoes and salad, served and cooked to perfection. Mrs. Kemeny suggested we drink bottled water rather than the local water. She had traveled around the world and said

that very often the local water in many areas would make a person ill if he were not accustomed to it. We had to pay for the bottled water (75¢ a bottle) as this was not included in the tour.

We were advised to get to bed early and reminded that we would be called at 3:30 A.M. Our luggage was to be outside our door by 4:00 A.M. so it could be picked up. I returned to my room, packed my baggage for the early morning departure, then crawled inside the huge mosquito netting arrangement to sleep.

Wednesday, Sept. 23

It seemed as though I had hardly gone to sleep when the telephone rang with a tremendous *beep* that shattered the stillness of the night. My tooth had begun to ache just as I lay down so I didn't get more than a couple hours sleep at most. I splashed some

Dakar's beautiful modern university.

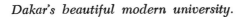

One of the moslems poses for a picture in a mosque at Dakar. The interior was so spotless that we had to remove our shoes to enter.

Our guide Hannah, standing in the mosque, attributes her sparkling white teeth to the small stick of wood she carries in her mouth. She rubs it against her teeth and gums like a toothbrush.

water on my face to wake up, stuck my luggage outside, gathered up my cameras and hand luggage, and went downstairs. I found my little pocket flashlight very useful in the early morning when groping about the strange hotel room and I slept with it beside my bed throughout the entire trip. It was now about 4:00 A.M. and slowly the group began to gather in the dining room for a light breakfast. We all ordered orange juice or coffee—the only two words that the waiters understood. The few in the group that knew French had not come down yet. Then the waiters held out their hand for money. We had no way of telling them that our meals were paid for by the tour and they insisted on payment. But then, no one could figure out how much to pay them. I didn't understand the local money at all and no matter how much I held out it was not right. Finally some of the people gave them a few dollar bills and this settled the situation. However, as soon as we got to the bus in front of the hotel Steve, our tour leader, found out about it, imme-

diately got the money back from the natives, and returned it to the tour members. It was simply a problem caused by a language barrier and we never had another problem over food. Steve told us that this early morning departure would be the only very early occasion of the whole trip, except on some of the game drives when we would be called at 5:30 in the morning.

We left Dakar at 5:30 A.M. by Pan American Jet Clipper and were soon settled comfortably in our seats. Our next stop would be Monrovia, Liberia, which we were told was originally founded by ex-slaves from America who were shipped back to Africa and resettled here. We stopped there only briefly and it was announced over the loudspeaker that anyone from South Africa would not be allowed to leave the plane. I got out for a quick look around as I wanted to see as much of Africa as possible and also to look for unusual souvenirs. Our next stop was Accra in Ghana, where we only stayed for a half hour. The

We leave Dakar for the long ride to Johannesburg, South Africa.

We stopped at a number of countries on the way to South Africa. I took this jungle scene from the window of the plane as we made a long, low sweep over the country at Lagos, Nigeria.

airport was very clean and modern—the most up-to-date airport I had seen so far in Africa. They had some interesting native handiwork for sale there but we didn't have much time to purchase anything. Next was Lagos, Nigeria, where I had my first glimpse of real jungle. The plane made a long, slow sweep over the area before landing at low altitude and as I looked out the window I saw a great deal of the surrounding area. The forests went from horizon to horizon. There were many palms mixed with immense trees that towered high above the jungle and small settlements of huts completely surrounded by the giant forests. It looked like it would have been an interesting place to visit. Before landing we flew just above the trees and I was able to get a fine view of the jungle growth.

They were apparently having some type of a war for it was announced over the loudspeaker that our plane would not be allowed to approach the terminal any closer than a half mile and that no photos could be taken. The stewardess told me that they would not guarantee our safety if we went ashore and that we would be safer on the plane so I stayed aboard. The plane was only stopping for a half hour so I felt that under the circumstances it wouldn't be worth the risk; besides it was raining. I saw a number of army troups parading outside with rifles, no doubt the small war or uprising was in the making with Biafra.

Our next stop was Kinshasa, formerly Léopoldville, in the Congo, where the same conditions prevailed as in Lagos. We were told not to take any photos or our cameras would be confiscated. I went into the terminal carrying my camera, as I didn't want to leave it on the plane, and hoped no one would try to take it away. However I didn't take any pictures. I saw a huge American B-52 bomber and a number of army troops, mostly white, which I felt were the freedom fighters paid for by the government. There were many beautiful ivory carvings for sale inside the building but they were very high priced and the natives would not come down on their price at all. Some of the tour members bought them. Our tour leader said that ivory items would be less expensive in Kenya than any place in Africa. The huge B-52 bomber, which took off just before us, was quite a spectacle. I noted similar bombers in two of the other airports that we had visited.

We only stayed here about a half hour, and soon were airborne on our way to South Africa! We flew at 33,000 feet and so far the flight had been very smooth. I was glad that I had sat by a window, for when the plane does go down to land as it had on our last three stops I was able to see a good amount of the country below. You can even take pictures as you fly over the land at low altitude just before landing. When I usually use a shutter speed of a 250th of a second to avoid camera movement and focus the camera at infinity, both movies and stills come out excellent if the light is good. You can also take some excellent photos while you are high up in the clouds, particularly movies. Some of the cloud formations are spectacular, especially when framed with the huge wing of your plane. Early morning sunrise or sunsets at high altitudes make wonderful endings for your home movies.

We had already passed over the equator and it was announced that we had also flown directly over Dr. Albert Schweitzer's famous hospital far below in the jungle. Today will be spent aboard the huge Pan American jet, traveling at over 600 miles per hour. That's how big Africa is! We will cover the entire continent from the extreme Western edge at Dakar, down along the Ivory Coast, through the Congo, across Angola, Botswana, to South Africa. There would be a total flying time of over 12 hours, compared with the early days of Stanley and Livingstone when the same

trip would have taken years on horseback. We had lunch and dinner aboard the plane en route, which were not quite as good as the food served on Stateside flights, chicken and rice several times with some type of whipped egg white for desert. But the flight and service were impeccable and most comfortable, except for the seats, which were a bit close for such a long sitting.

We had been flying since 5:30 in the morning, except for our brief stops on the Ivory Coast, and we were now approaching Johannesburg. It was night time and the city lights were visible through the windows on both sides of the plane, as far as the eye could see. It was a thrilling sight. We landed smoothly and taxied up to the terminal.

3. South Africa—Johannesburg—Kruger Park

We had just landed in Johannesburg, South Africa, at 9:00 P.M. We were instructed to stay in our seats until the health officer boarded the plane to check our passports and to see if we had the proper shots. We also had to fill out two questionnaires for entry into the country, listing passport number, name, nationality, etc. Once the health officer looked at our passports and the attached health cards, checking each one carefully, we left the plane. The outside temperature was a cool 58 degrees. As soon as we got into the terminal Steve suggested that we purchase South African money—at least $20 worth—so we would have money to spend in the country. Meanwhile, while we were exchanging our American dollars he checked our luggage and collected our passports, showing us how to insert the forms we had filled out so we could go through immigration quickly. He handled all the details for us and we simply walked through a gate where a man stamped our passports. In a matter of minutes we were ready to go to the hotel. I must emphasize how simple a long trip can be when you go by guided tour, instead of trying to do it on your

own. Our tour leader, Mr. Chering, handled all matters in a most expert way with no delay whatsoever.

We boarded the bus that had been waiting for us and were just about to start when Steve (Mr. Chering) made an announcement. He said that he had told us earlier that he had never lost a single piece of luggage. Well now his record was broken and he had *finally* lost a bag—his own! He said he was telling it like a joke to keep from *crying*, but that the airlines would eventually find it. The bus left the terminal headed for the hotel. We went about eight miles when the bus slowly coasted to a stop. Then came the futile attempt of trying to start the motor and the anticipated running down of the battery. The driver got out of the bus and walked to a nearby hotel to phone for taxis, as our hotel was still 12 miles away. Finally, after waiting for over an hour, a single taxi drove up and after considerable consultation with the bus driver and our tour leader, they began loading our luggage into the cab. Then more waiting. Finally after what seemed an eternity, two more cabs came—one driven by a beautiful girl with long, shoulder-length, brown hair. I rode in her cab and I must admit she was a good driver. (She said she was the only woman cab driver in the whole town.) About a half hour later we reached the President Hotel, right in the very center of Johannesburg, which is probably the biggest, the best, and the most modern hotel in South Africa, perhaps even in all of Africa.

We walked inside, and because all reservations had been arranged by the tour we were immediately given our room number and keys. My room, on the seventh floor, was beautiful, with thick rugs and a spotless interior. There were welcome signs everywhere; two telephones, one by the bed and one in the luxurious bathroom; special scented soaps and silver soap dishes; an insulated pitcher of ice water; many handsome towels in the bath; gold embossed stationery; and my own little private balcony outside the room, overlooking the city. The bed was very comfortable with warm blankets that guarded against the cool air. Because the city is located at a high altitude the temperature is perfect in the daytime and a little cool at night. I could hear the wind whistle about the tall building outside.

Thursday, Sept. 25

It was now 12:30 P.M. We had arrived at the hotel quite late due to the bus breakdown. My luggage had been delivered to my room and after I laid out my gear for the next day's trip to Kruger Park, I took a bath and crawled into the warm bed. I was thoroughly exhausted, not having more than four hours sleep in the last three days. I put my head down on the comfortable pillow and was just about to drop off to sleep when my tooth started aching and it felt like my whole head was coming loose. I could hardly stand the pain, let alone sleep. I had found out earlier, that the only thing that would relieve the pain was ice water, so I would take a sip of ice water and then try to sleep. But if I swallowed the water the devastating pain would slowly creep back, increasing in intensity every second in a rising crescendo of torture. I gulped down aspirins, pain killers, then sipped more ice water. I was so tired, I wanted nothing more than to sleep. I would try to sleep holding a mouthful of water but the moment I would start to doze off, my mouth would pop open and the water would spill out. Then the pain would build up to maximum torture and I would grab frantically for the ice water. I must have gotten in and out of bed at least a hundred times. I watched the hours go by—1:30, 2:30, 3:30—and felt so alone in a strange city, half way around the world. I was getting desperate. I took out the X-rays that the dentist had given me in Miami and studied the abscess area. If I could open a small place near the tooth perhaps I could let the infection drain, I thought.

I had a small, very sharp, stainless-steel pocket knife that I felt I could do the job with. I tried to shine my flashlight into my mouth and at the same time hold it open wide. The only trouble was I only had two hands. One time I cut my lip with the razor-sharp knife; the next time I stuck the blade into the wrong tooth. I decided to abandon the operation and stick with the ice water. It began to look like my entire vacation would be spoiled because of a lousy toothache. The brochure for the tour had mentioned a precautionary trip to the dentist and how I wish I had heeded this advice. I thought of skipping the Kruger Park trip and seeking out a local dentist. We were scheduled to get up at 7:30 A.M. and it was now almost 5:00.

It seemed as though I had just closed my eyes when the phone rang. Time to get up! I stumbled over to the mirror, splashed some water on my face, and proceeded to shave. Then the doorbell rang. It was time to put my large suitcase outside the door. We had been advised to take just our small handbag with a change of clothes and our toilet articles with us to the park as there would be limited facilities there and on the small vehicles in which we would travel. The larger suitcases would be checked at the hotel and we would get them upon our return. This same procedure was to follow throughout the whole trip. We were also told to wear our oldest clothes in the park, which was very informal and quite dusty. I finished dressing and went down to the lobby loaded down with my three cameras and my bulging shoulder bag. Most of the group had already gathered in the lobby, and some of them were going to Cape Town instead of Kruger, an optional part of the tour. They would join us again back at the same hotel after their trip. Steve was busy getting everyone off and tending to baggage. I was glad to hear that his lost suitcase had finally been located. My tooth was hurting very little and things were beginning to look up a bit. Then Steve said there would be a half hour delay so I decided to have breakfast.

The breakfast room was on the third floor overlooking the swimming pool, which was surrounded by a beautiful lawn. A cute, mini-skirted waitress named Doris took my order of two eggs, sausage, juice, rolls, toast, and coffee (a whole pot). Steve had a few spare minutes so he joined me for breakfast, which was served very quickly and was excellent. We signed tickets for our meals. I couldn't remember my room number and Steve couldn't remember his either. It had been a hectic night for both of us. Then we went

Our guide at Kruger Park was Charlie Walton (right). The gentleman in the center is Steven Chering, our Percival guide for the entire African trip.

movie of the gate with its sign and we drove inside.

Kruger National Park, one of the oldest and largest national parks in Africa, is approximately 200 miles long and varies in width from 30 to 60 miles, with a total area of 7,340 square miles. It was established in 1926 to protect the dwindling wildlife of South Africa. I had looked forward to visiting this famous park ever since I had first read about it. Now at last I was here.

We had hardly driven through the gates when we started seeing all kinds of animals—impala, wildebeest, sable antelopes, baboons, and guinea fowl. It was almost dark so we had to move on to the rest camp, since we had to be inside the gates to the camp also by

down to the lobby and joined the others waiting for the trip to Kruger. The group was divided into two small, very neat, Volkswagen buses, which were painted with black and white zebra stripes. Our driver, Charles Walton, formerly of England, has lived in South Africa for 23 years and loves it. It was a long drive from Jo-burg (the short name for Johannesburg, used locally). At first the ride was rather monotonous but it picked up in beauty and interest as the trip progressed. At first glance the countryside looks much like pastoral New England, with newly plowed fields and small herds of cattle and sheep. But then the road becomes hilly with tropical aloes similar to the Southwest desert land.

We saw our first wild game, a large herd of blesbok that a farmer was keeping on his land. He had allowed them to live there in peace for many years, right along with his cattle and sheep. This was the only wild game we saw on the entire trip from Jo-burg to the gates of Kruger Park. All the other game has long ago been killed off by relentless hunting and killing in the past 60 years. There were a few small orange groves scattered throughout the hills and small stands of sugar cane in the low areas. All road signs (and practically every other sign in the area) are printed in both English and Afrikaans, the native dialect.

The long ride to the park, about 150 miles, gave us an excellent chance to see the country in the comfortable mini-buses. After stopping at a nice restaurant for lunch, we drove on to the park. Our guide said that we must be inside the park by 6:00 P.M. or they would close the gates and we wouldn't be able to get in. When we finally reached the gates I made a short

The rest camps at Kruger Park were very clean and decorated with pretty flowers. Each hut was air-conditioned and had a private bath.

This rare photo shows the Klipspringer antelope poised on a huge boulder and outlined against the evening sky at Kruger Park.

This graceful impala was the first animal we saw at Kruger.

6:00 P.M. or the driver of our bus would be heavily fined. He told us that they fine safari guides heavily for each minute past the deadline. We arrived at the Pretorius Kop Rest Camp just a little before six and were quickly assigned to our huts. Each unit was round, built like a native hut with grass thatched roof, and surprisingly, air-conditioned. Since we were all very hungry after the long drive we placed our hand luggage in our rooms and rushed off to the dining room, which did not stay open very late. We had a delicious choice of lobster, beef, or fish, and potatoes, greens, rolls, and dessert was served with the meal.

After dinner, I promptly returned to my hut for rest. We had to get up at 5:30 A.M. for our early morning game drive and I was utterly exhausted, having had practically no sleep in four days. I was so tired, I didn't even notice that I had a bathroom and shower right in my hut. I had walked around the camp with my flashlight looking for the restrooms and when I couldn't find them I came back to my hut and promptly

dropped off to sleep—my first good night's sleep on the trip.

Friday, Sept. 26

We were awakened at 5:30 for our early morning game drive, which was fascinating. We would drive slowly along the road at about 15 mph and all eyes would search the woods for game. The animals would be seen just a few feet in from the edge of the road. We first came across large numbers of impala, which were seen at every turn (there are an estimated 180,-000 of them in the park). Then we saw a small group of wart hogs with their young, a large flock of guinea fowl, and further on a troupe of baboons. Our guide would not move on until everyone was finished taking pictures.

Next we saw a great number of small hornbills, strange birds with huge bills, which spend much of their time on the ground. Because they were com-

We saw impala at every turn and never tired of looking at them. There are about 180,000 of them in the park.

pletely unafraid they walked right up to our bus (probably looking for a free handout) and we could take good close-up movies of them. In fact all the animals were so accustomed to cars that we could easily approach them within 20 or 30 feet before they ran away. We saw kudu, zebra, and then a huge giraffe, who just stood by the side of the road watching us, posing perfectly for a picture. He was a brilliant orange and white, very exciting for color photography. As we drove on we saw more giraffe, a huge elephant feeding by the water, buffalo, and crocodiles. We saw a crocodile snapping at impala as they came down to the water to drink. I thought they would leave but they stayed right there and drank. They stood far back from the water and reached their heads forward as far as possible taking a drink from the first inch or two of water, ready to leap back instantly. It was an interesting sight.

We came across more and more giraffe and finally hippo—a whole herd of them basking in the river. We couldn't get close enough to them for photos however. In Kruger you are not allowed to get out of your car under any circumstances, and all photography must be done from within the car. As long as you stay inside

you are completely safe from all the animals except elephants, which must be approached with great caution as they can easily tip over a car. The impala were behind every bush and every turn of the road. They were totally unafraid as they stood right in the center of the road, almost daring the driver to run them over. Sometimes he would have to slow down or apply the brakes to keep from hitting them as they walked in front of us, completely unconcerned.

We hadn't had breakfast yet, and everyone was hungry, so we pulled into the Skukuza Rest Camp for breakfast. This rest camp was more beautiful than the first. The patio and restaurant overlooked a large waterhole, where there were about 50 impala and kudu cavorting about the grassy bank, drinking and grazing. We could watch this pretty sight while eating a breakfast of bacon and eggs, orange juice, mealy-meal (ground corn with milk), curry-mince (ground meat), toast, and coffee—all you wanted. Everything was cooked just fine and tasted especially good after our early morning drive.

After breakfast—more game viewing. We saw many more giraffe that were so easy to photograph. They would simply stand alongside the road and look at us

A large baboon sitting beside the road at Kruger Park.

The thatched roof of the rondeval "huts" is not only attractive but it makes the interior comfortable. This one is under construction.

Huge wart hogs were common throughout the park.

We saw many giraffe, and each view of them was worth a photo or movie footage.

while we took their picture. Then we saw a large baboon riding on top of a car. He finally jumped off and ran back to his group. We didn't see any lions but we did see a leopard sleeping on a low branch of a huge, leafy tree. He would have been completely hidden from view except that his long tail hung straight down from the branch. He was in the shade and we couldn't photograph him but it was exciting to look at him through binoculars. Many visitors here never see leopards as the park is practically all wooded, making it difficult to spot them because of the dense brush. We saw a very large herd of buffalo, across the far bank of the river, and there were some huge gray animals among them that we were told were white rhinos. The park has a number of these huge beasts and they are considered the second largest animal on land, next only to the elephant. They are much larger than the more common black rhino and may stand six feet or more high at the shoulder. We could not get close to them so we watched them with binoculars.

Baboons were very common as were small but beautiful vervet monkeys. We rounded a bend in the road and saw some enormous black birds on the ground ahead. We drove right up to them. They were a species of Ground Hornbills and were as big as a full-sized turkey. Their huge beaks measured close to a foot in

The female kudu lacks the horns of the male but is none the less just as spectacular.

length and they had a bright red marking on their heads. They dug into the ground for berries or grubs, which they would gulp down, paying little attention to us. Everywhere we saw many giant ant hills—some six to ten feet high! The grass in the entire area was bone dry and lifeless and the trees were almost com-

pletely bare of leaves. We were in the park in the dry season when most of the trees shed their leaves just as they do in winter in the Northern part of our own country. The park was not as scenic for photography as it would be after the rainy season when everything would be bright green, but we were told that this is

A small herd of impala drinking along the river at the Skukuza Rest Camp.

trol" them. They call it "cropping"; I call it slaughter. We drove over large areas of the park where we would not see a single animal. Considering that the park has over 7,000 square miles, it would appear to me that there is a better answer to "protecting" the animals in a game preserve than killing them. After all, the animals were the *only* reason any of us came to the park. We have plenty of woods back home. I heard from some of the local people that so many animals had been killed off in Kruger Park in the name of cropping that its animal population has been vastly reduced and that the game officials are now trying to buy animals from other animal parks to replenish their stock. Without the animals, Kruger Park will cease to be a tourist attraction.

There were a great many impala in the park and giraffe were also numerous but still we saw no lions, and Kruger is supposed to be famous for its lions. We saw a few more elephants in the distance but they were so far away that we had to use binoculars just to see them. The sun was getting low in the sky and more and more game seemed to be waking up. The very best time see game is an hour or two before sunset. You will usually see more activity at this time than at any other time of the day. We saw nine giraffe in one spot, all calmly grazing at the top of

the best time to see the animals that would otherwise be hidden in the dense foliage.

I noted that many trees had been tipped over or were broken in half—the work of elephants. They do this when they are feeding and it is said that a large herd can easily devastate a wooded area in short order. There is a little controversy about this as to whether or not it is harmful to the terrain. Some naturalists become alarmed about it and advocate the shooting of the elephants, keeping their number down to a low level. Other naturalists take just the opposite view. They see the toppling of trees as a natural effort that benefits all the animals and the area as well. When the tree is uprooted, new grass grows in the disturbed area. The fallen trees eventually rot and fertilize the other trees. Thus the elephant thins out the dense trees and brush, allowing a little grass to grow which of course benefits the smaller grazing animals. I certainly agree with this. I think too many park rangers and ecologists are too quick with the gun, thinking that shooting animals in the parks is the best way to "con-

As we rounded a bend in the road we sighted this enormous black bird, a species of ground hornbill, that was as large as a turkey.

Cute vervet monkeys were fairly common throughout the park. Someone gave this fellow an orange.

some trees that still had their leaves. Giraffe were easy to locate because they are so tall they can hardly hide. I think they are among the most spectacular of animals, second only to the elephant and lion.

Keenly searching for lions, we stopped several times in areas where a lion had just been sighted but we couldn't see any. In Kruger, when any car stops alongside the road, it is usually a sign that the driver has spotted something so other cars stop also to look. Sometimes it may be a false alarm and six or eight cars will stop, all eyes gazing intently into the bush, only to find that the first car hadn't seen anything at all. He had stopped simply to take a drink of water from a picnic jug! But usually if a car stopped there was something there to see. This was how we had seen the leopard. A car had stopped and the driver pointed it out to us. The woods actually give the park

a sense of mystery and discovery, for if the area was all open land, you wouldn't have to search for the animals and the thrill of discovery would be lost. I think it is one of the most rewarding features of Kruger—the search for the animals and the excitement of discovering them lurking among the trees.

I would like to have seen large herds of elephants, especially at close range. I had always envisioned huge herds of elephant in Kruger Park and was disappointed that I did not see them. I hope they have not been wantonly slaughtered on the advice of some ecologist who is more worried about the trees than he is the animals. Perhaps the large herds are in some other area of the park. Due to the enormous land area of the park, I am sure we saw only a tiny portion of it. I would also like to have seen hippo up close. The ones we saw were too far away to photograph. Also of course, I missed seeing a single lion.

We crossed the Sabie River and climbed a high hill where we could look down into a huge valley and see for miles around. We could see giraffe and kudu coming down to drink in a small man-made lake, where the river had been dammed to conserve the water during the dry season. The sun was getting low in the sky so we headed back to the Skukuza Rest Camp for a much needed rest and dinner. It had been a most beautiful and interesting day. The weather was perfect, the temperature a comfortable 75 degrees, although it was a trifle cool in the morning and after sundown. We reached camp at sundown and after a shower and shave, I washed out a shirt and a few clothes so I wouldn't run short on the trip. Then I went to dinner.

Our group usually ate together at one large table or several smaller ones. The first one to sit at a table would soon be joined by others in the group so that no one would have to eat alone. We could order anything on the menu and we usually selected different items so that by the time we left an area, we would have tried everything on the menu. I thought the food was excellent but some of the group didn't think it was especially good. We were told that the early morning game drive for tomorrow had been canceled. Most of the group had decided that they had seen enough game and didn't want to bother with the early morning drive. I was very disappointed for the itinerary called for the drive and I felt that I had come 8,000 miles to see the animals. Also I would probably

Strange trees and bushes hide the animals from poachers.

Hand-carved rhino and elephant from Kruger National Park in South Africa.

never get a chance to see Kruger Park again and the excursion the next morning would have given me a chance to see a little more of the area. But I could also see the viewpoint of the group. It had been a very long hard ride from Jo-Burg to the park; it had been a long hard day on the game drive; then it would be a long hard drive back to Jo-Burg, uphill all the way. Everyone was just plain tired.

Saturday, Sept. 27

We left the rest camp at 9:00 A.M. after a hearty breakfast. As we rushed out of the park we saw little game. Again I felt sad for I would have liked to make the one more drive through the area as originally planned. We saw a few zebra and giraffe but didn't stop as the driver wanted to get back to Jo-Burg. I could see his point as we drove back, for the trip was mostly uphill since the city is at a high altitude. It takes a great deal longer to make the trip back and it

is a hard day's drive. I noted again that after we left the gates of the park there was absolutely no wild game, not even so much as a rabbit, all the way back to town. Practically all of the land between Jo-Burg and the park is under cultivation and both the white and native hunters have long ago eradicated all game. In some areas there would be mile upon mile of slender trees with loose bark. I was told that these were especially cultivated for the huge tannery in South Africa that uses the bark in the tanning process. A huge tannery in Cape Town is said to be one of the largest in all Africa.

There were a number of small native huts or shacks along the roadside. We were informed that the farmers allow the natives to build the huts on their land and that the natives then work for the farmer and usually settle down for life. The landscape was dotted with pretty orange groves. In one area there was even a drive-in theatre and I noticed that there were roadside parks along the highway just like in the States. The highway itself was very good and traffic was light. If it weren't for the fact that we were driving on the left side of the road and that the road signs were in two languages, it was almost like being home. Coca-cola and Shell signs were common and the homes were of similar construction to those found in our own country.

The trip to and from Kruger used up two full days. If we had spent two full days viewing the game I would have been happy but the one day is just not enough considering the long drive just to get there. I understand they are initiating a new jet plane service to the park. You could drive one way by bus, then fly back. This way you could have the full two days to view the game and avoid the long, slow return trip.

We stopped at the Crocodile Motel for lunch, a beautiful place with 40 acres of orange groves, a swim-ming pool, and beautiful gardens with many flowers. I had a fillet steak that was tender and delicious, a salad, vegetables, rolls, and dessert. Everything was done to perfection. Again I was impressed with the tour and the fact that we stopped at such wonderful places to eat or rest. Then we continued on to Jo-Burg, which we were told is located at an altitude of 6,000 feet.

It was sad that in the hundreds of miles of beautiful, hilly land on both sides of the road not a single head of wild game could be seen, especially since the area teemed with wildlife in the last century. Except for the small herds of antelope on the one farmer's land there was no game whatsoever outside of the preserve. One would think that the government would allow the animals to come back and re-build their herds in these civilized times so that tourists could see animals when

One of the most beautiful views on our trip was seen from the Crocodile Motel grounds.

they drive about the country. If they became too numerous they could be hunted, but to wipe them out completely was shocking to me. I had expected to see all kinds of wild animals as soon as I left the outskirts of the city. Now, from what I have seen, I wonder if the animals are not being killed off *right inside the park*, for fear that there might be too many of them. Of course our country has done the very same thing with the bison and most of its game but I had expected Africa to be all wild animals. I think that the governments should allow the animals to increase outside the game preserves as well as in them. If they get rid of the animals this will be getting rid of their unique attraction and tourists will visit other more accessible areas of the world. I noted that the farmer who kept the antelope on his land was using only a four-foot-high cattle fence, yet the animals stayed on his land. Kruger had used a six-foot fence at least on one side to keep the animals from going into the inhabited areas. We were told that the animals quickly learn to stay inside their protected area as they learn they are less likely to be shot at there.

We stopped to use restrooms at a filling station. The driver asked the attendants if the toilets were clean, as this was standard procedure. The natives tending the station assured us that they were. You must pay a penny to get inside, which is the same throughout the area. It certainly was a long grind back to Jo-Burg. We came across a huge steel mill and it spewed out so much smoke from its buildings that it turned day into night. Air pollution at its worst! The driver could hardly see the road it was so bad. Then we no sooner left the terribly polluted area than we encountered fierce dust storms, which again reduced visibility to just a few feet. We had to shut all windows tightly to avoid asphyxiation. It was now getting late and darkness had set in. When we finally reached the city at 7:00 P.M., after a hard full day's drive, it started to rain.

We arrived at the President Hotel and were immediately assigned our rooms. After first cleaning up and putting on a coat and tie (meals are formal at the hotel), we had dinner. I had fillet steak again with a baked potato, salad, rolls, and the works. The desserts were especially good as we had a choice of all kinds of tempting cakes, puddings, and fruit salads. Everything was so delicious that we all ate too much. After dessert they brought around a huge assortment of cheeses and crackers and you could try a slice or two of as many as you liked. I sat with Mrs. Eva Gall and other members of the group and after dinner, leaving the table a little stuffed, we decided to walk around the town to help settle the meal.

We had been cautioned that it was not safe to walk the streets at night, especially alone, so we decided to stay close to the downtown area. We had only gone two blocks when we noticed that we were in a very rough-looking area. There were numerous drunks, yelling and hollering as they staggered down the street. I was a little apprehensive in passing them but they paid no attention to us. They were black Africans, probably celebrating pay day. Our guide on the Kruger trip had explained to us that the native blacks are called Afrikans. The mixed races, where blacks have married whites, especially in the early days of settlement, are called the Colored. This includes all the other races, the Chinese, the Indians, everyone except the white Caucasians or Europeans, who are called the Whites.

There were many people on the streets but this was probably because it was Saturday night. The whole city was very modern and it made you feel like you were in the U.S., until someone gave you directions with the charming British accent. I purchased a Sunday newspaper to read before going to bed that night. I thought it would be interesting to read the South African version of what was happening in their country.

It was getting late so we returned to the hotel. All of the stores were closed in the city (they close from Saturday noon to Monday morning), which sort of put a crimp on our souvenir shopping. But we had been able to buy a few items at the gift shops in Kruger. I bought some postcards at the hotel and wrote a number of them to my family and friends back home. They mailed them for me right at the hotel, affixing the proper stamps, and the problem of buying stamps and figuring out the money was eliminated. I enjoyed reading the paper immensely, particularly the editorial and letters to the editor section, which provided an insight into the thinking of the general population. There was little mention of the U.S. in the papers. I had thought our country would figure prominently in the news but it was mostly about South Africa. There was considerable debate about television which is absolutely banned in the whole country as the present government considers it degrading. I can't say as I disagree with them for I think TV leaves a lot to be desired. I know I didn't miss it at all on the entire trip. There was also an article about Kruger Park in it. Some people are going to build a new game preserve on 50,000 acres right next to the park and stock it with numerous animals. They will build a hotel in the center and keep the entire area primitive so that visitors to the preserve will see Africa as it was in the last century. They said that Kruger had become too commercial with its tar roads and numerous rest camps. Also they said the animal population was down. I agreed with them from the little I had seen of the park.

It was now well past midnight. I opened the glass door to my little private balcony and looked out over the city. The air was very chilly and crisp but I en-joyed it. I could hear drunks yelling in the quiet of the night. There seemed to be quite a few of them. My tooth started to ache again so I gulped down about five aspirins and then dropped off to sleep. I must admit that it was exciting to visit South Africa. In fact everything about the trip was fascinating to me.

Close-up of one of the strange trees in the park.

We saw a tree with strange fruit. Upon closer inspection, the clumps of "fruit" turned out to be baboons!

A picturesque Acacia Tree loaded down with nests from the Weaver Bird.

A giant Kudu partly hidden by the dense bush. It is this dense brush that adds mystery and discovery to game viewing at Kruger Park, for you must actively search for the animals. They are not out in the open as in some parks.

Sunday, Sept. 28

Today we go to the Mine Dances. We thought it might rain, as it had rained briefly in the early evening, but the skies were bright and clear and a chill was in the air. We boarded a large sight-seeing bus and headed for the gold mines.

We were told that the mine dances are held to provide recreation for the Bantu mineworkers who labor in the hot gold mines all week. They give the workers a chance to relieve their tensions after working hard. Admission to the dance is by written invitation only and we were each presented with our own special note. Today the dance was held at the Durban Roodepoort Deep, but each time it is held at a different mine. We were fortunate that this particular mine was quite close to town, as sometimes they may be a hundred or more miles away. Our special invitation gave

a brief account of the dances and also contained instructions and regulations for those attending: do not wear bathing suits, do not enter the dance arena, don't throw money to the dancers, do not enter any part of the living quarters, other than the dance stands. We had hardly left town when we saw a sign pointing to the mine and soon we were at the gates. A beautiful shrubbery-and-flower-decked road led into it.

The dance was held in a small circular arena and it was attended by approximately a thousand people— about half black and half white. The blacks sat on one side and the whites the other, as mingling of the races is not allowed in South Africa. As soon as we sat down the colorful dances began. The natives, dressed in animal skins with colorful feathers and ornaments, played primitive musical instruments. It would have been nice to have a recording of the interesting music. Some of the dance groups brought along their own orchestra

The famous Mine Dance at Johannesburg was a colorful and exciting event open to tour members only by special invitation by the mines.

A gaily dressed native doing the Mine Dance.

which consisted of handmade wooden xylophones that gave out a marvelous sound. The drums were made from empty 55-gallon oil drums with a skin tied tightly over the top. I was amazed at the beautiful music the natives produced with such primitive equipment. One of the groups played the *Sarie Marais,* the most popular folk song named after a girl. We sat by a fifth generation white African, who explained many of the dances to us and told us that the white Europeans are invited only once a month.

Each dance was quite interesting and varied considerably from the last. A sign with the name and number of the dance was posted as each started so that the audience could properly identify it. Natives from the audience would often participate in the dance by letting out a long, piercing catcall. The rhythm of the old drums made from animal hides and the sounds from the strange instruments added a pleasing background to the colorful dances. I wished that I had brought along a tape recorder but you just can't carry everything on a trip to Africa. One lady from the group did bring along a recorder and she said that while trying to take movies and record the music, she had missed large portions of the dance. I found my three

The industrial section of Jo-Burg (short name for Johannesburg) is surrounded by huge mine dumps, a by-product of the gold mines.

cameras more than enough to handle. I would take movies of each dance group, then quickly pick up my still camera with the telephoto lens for closeup shots. Then I would take a picture or two, set the camera down, and reach for my other camera with the wide-angle lens. I wanted to get over-all shots showing the entire scene in addition to the close-ups. The two still cameras worked perfectly and I would recommend that anyone going to Africa bring two cameras. Not only was I able to have the advantage of a four-inch telephoto lens in one and an extreme wide angle in the other—an ideal combination for photography—but I had the assurance of two cameras for my trip. It is so easy for a camera to suddenly stop working due to a slight malfunction of the shutter or winding mechanism.

I had thought the dances would go on all day but they ended rather suddenly and everyone started to leave. There was a small souvenir stand on the premises where I was able to purchase a program of the dances. They also had full length records of the dance music but I was afraid it would get broken on the long journey ahead, so I didn't buy one. As the crowd quickly dispersed I noted that some of the dancers were posing for photos and charging a slight fee as usual.

We boarded the bus and headed back to town. On the way we stopped at various parts of the mine to take photos. Our guide explained that they are very deep, some going to 13,000 feet down into the ground. I would like to have gone down into the mine itself but was told that this is quite dangerous. You can visit a mine but it is rather complicated to make the arrangements, and women aren't allowed down in the shafts at all. The heat is tremendous due to the great depths. We were told that it takes roughly a ton of ore to produce an ounce of gold. The ore is treated with cyanide, which extracts all of the gold from it and gives it a gold color. Then the discarded ore is piled into huge, pyramid-like hills—mine dumps—out-side the mine. Because they were using up valuable land, they were becoming quite a problem until sud-denly someone discovered a way to make beautiful yellow building blocks from the discarded ore. Now each mine dump can be converted into millions of building blocks and the formerly useless dumps have suddenly become more valuable than the gold that was extracted from them. After we were shown the

Each group of mine dancers was trying to outdo the other. These dancers wore bells attached to their chests and by rapid vibrations of the chest muscles they would ring in unison.

small ore cars that carry the ore from the mine shaft into the processing plants we then headed back to the hotel.

We had been eating such huge meals lately I wasn't very hungry. I decided to eat in the grill, a more casual dining room on the third floor of the hotel. They had a beautiful smorgasbord of fine foods spread out on several tables, with every kind of meat, fish, cheese, seafood, and snack that you could imagine. The desserts were equally tempting. I ate a huge dinner, despite the fact that I wasn't hungry and had planned to eat lightly that evening. I dined with several members of our group.

We walked around the hotel after dinner to look at the dining rooms and to decide which we would choose for our next meal. They have about five or six main dining rooms: the Gold Room, the Silver Room, the Platinum Room, the Diamond Room, and the Transvaal Room. There is another on the 25th floor but we never got up to see it. One of the guests said that it had a magnificent view of the entire city, especially at night. All of the dining rooms are formal

This native sword dance is full of action.

No race mixing is allowed in South Africa. Spectators to an event are separated by a railing accordingly.

except for the grill where we had breakfast and lunch. However at night, you are expected to wear coat and tie here also.

Money in South Africa is not too difficult to understand. The *rand,* which is our equivalent of the dollar, is worth $1.40, so that a five rand bill is worth about $7.00. They use pennies, nickels, and dimes, and each is worth a little more than our own coins. I purchased $20 worth of South African money and found that it was all I needed for our stay there.

After lunch we boarded a bus for our afternoon tour of the city. We had been requested not to talk politics with the local guide or bus driver, but everyone began asking questions about the country and its govern-

ment. We were told that the trains in South Africa are driven only by Europeans but the buses are driven by both whites and non-whites. The non-whites have their own buses, taxies, schools, swimming pools, etc. Many of the Afrikaans and coloreds work in the mines. They work a straight eight-hour day and are given free medical treatment and hospitalization. They usually work on a contract of six, nine, or twelve months, and after their term is completed, they are sent home for a few months to rest. To insure that they arrive with all of their hard-earned money, the government escorts each of them home with their pay and deposits it in the bank. All of the local white people feel that despite the fact that the races are rigidly divided the black people there are very happy. They have their own schools, even universities, and are encouraged to work among their own when they graduate as doctors or lawyers.

We visited the site of the first gold mine to be discovered in South Africa in the year 1866. The mine is no longer in use and the open shaft is fenced so that people won't try to go down inside. We were told that there are about 40 gold mines in the Jo-Burg area and giant mine dumps all over. One man bought a dump and flattened it on the top where he built an outdoor drive-in theatre. We drove up on it and were treated to a magnificent view of the city. I could imagine that at night when the theatre was in operation the view of the city lights must be superb.

We noted huge clouds of dust blowing across the city from the exposed sand of the many mine dumps. Then we drove on to visit other areas of the city. We saw the colored sections of town where the Bantu and colored people live. They have their own schools, churches and cemeteries. The colored in Africa are not the same as the colored in the U.S. In Africa the colored are considered a mixture of white and native African. The original colored population there came from the early Dutch settlers who took up with native women. The Bantu are native Black Afrikans. They are allowed to marry the colored but, according to the laws of the country, a white cannot marry either a colored or a Bantu or he will be deported immediately from the country. The Chinese are classified as colored while the Japanese are classified as white. The government is extremely strict about races. The birth certificate of a person determines in which part of the city he must live, according to his nationality and family history. It was all quite complicated.

We saw some local Bantu women carrying heavy loads balanced on their heads and were told that they can carry as much as 180 pounds. They can carry an eight-gallon jug of water for miles without spilling a drop. They are taught to balance things on their heads from the time they are two years old.

As we toured most of the city we saw many beautiful· buildings, lovely parks, and a thousand-acre zoo, which is considered to be one of the finest in the world. I would like to have visited it instead of looking at more buildings but we just drove by. The highways were clean and well kept and there were many fine homes, as pretty as anyone would find in the States. They have an ultra-modern railroad station where all the trains enter the terminal two or three stories below the ground so that you neither see nor hear them. Also there were many new skyscrapers being con-

structed all over the city. Our tour was not only interesting but educational as well. However, I still would have preferred to spend the extra day in Kruger seeing the animals and would gladly have given up both the mine dance and the tour of the city.

We arrived back at the hotel fairly early and I took a quick shower and shave. We have a big day ahead of us tomorrow. I noticed a string sticking out of the wall over the bath tub. At first I was hesitant to touch it for I thought it might summon the bellboy, but then I pulled and out came a clothesline! It had a clip on it so that it could attach to the other end of the tub on the wall. The President people think of everything! I washed out a few of my clothes and hung them out to dry. It only took a few minutes and I found that if you didn't do this, you would soon have a bundle of soiled clothes to carry with you.

Several new people had joined us at Jo-Burg and we now had 22 on our tour. The group consisted mostly of elderly widows or middle-aged married couples. A few were in their 40s like myself and one or two were younger. Apparently these tours are catered to largely by older people as they are probably the only ones who can afford it. A younger man had joined the group at Jo-Burg, and there was also one other man younger than I who had gone on the Cape Town trip. I would have preferred traveling with people my own age, as I felt a little out of place, but I had come to Africa to see and photograph animals—not to meet people. Most were very nice, although there was a little friction between some of them. One lady threatened to let another have it "right in the kisser" if she so much as opened her mouth. Little tensions can build up on a trip because a group is together so long—sort of like living on an island with a small number of people. Certain things they do irritate you because you see them so often. Many would complain about the food, and some of the women would be unhappy if the tour director did not sit with them. He had to be ever so careful to divide his time evenly among the group. I thought he did a marvelous job as it is very difficult to cater to the wishes of a mixed group of people.

Tomorrow morning we leave for Zambia and have a big day ahead of us. I repacked my suitcase, which was requested to be put outside our room by a certain time so that it could be collected and loaded on the bus. I noted that my film was going fast. I had already taken about 200 still pictures and eight rolls of movie film. Then I carefully repacked my small hand bag to carry with me on the plane. I wanted everything ready for the next day so that I wouldn't have to rush in the early morning. Then I went down to dinner for my last evening meal in Jo-Burg. I ate in the Transvaal Room on the first floor with Trudy Kemeny, John Corbey, and Rose Meinhardt. We ate nearly all of our meals together. This was a very fancy dining room with well-dressed waiters and a wall-to-floor painting of early English scenes. The dinner was superb. I had delicious shrimp, potatoes, salad, marvelous cheeses, and desserts. We had a great deal of difficulty in getting water to drink, however, as the waiters are almost insulted if you ask for water instead of wine. My tooth began to ache at almost every meal and water was the only thing that would soothe it. Because it was Sunday night, and the hotel was completely filled, service was a little slower than usual. But it was an excellent meal and we all vowed to eat less "next time." We wanted to walk around the town a little to settle our dinner but my tooth started aching so I excused myself and went up to my room. I swallowed several aspirin and finally went off to sleep.

Monday, Sept. 29

Today we leave for Zambia! I was supposed to have an early breakfast in my room but it never came because I didn't put my room number on the card. Finally after waiting I went down to the grill for my last breakfast in South Africa. Jo-Burg is a nice city and the President Hotel is fabulous but I was glad to leave. I came to Africa to see animals, not buildings or cities, and wished that I had spent the time in Kruger Park that we had spent in the city. I would certainly recommend that anyone going there should fly from Jo-Burg so that they can spend a full two or three days in the park itself. But that's all water over the dam now.

We boarded the bus outside the hotel at 9:00 A.M. and headed for the airport, where we had about an

We rode South African Airlines to Rhodesia. The inside of the plane was decorated with leaping impala.

hour and a half wait until the plane took off at 11:00. Our South African Airlines 727 Boeing Stratojet had walls decorated with impala, African flowers, and zebras. A light lunch was served—which reminds me, if you plan to lose weight on one of these tours, forget it! You will be loaded down with so much delicious food from morning to night that your diet will be ruined. It's difficult to turn down such delicious food.

I said goodbye to South Africa as our jet carried us swiftly away. I chuckled to myself as I remembered our last night at the hotel. It seems that some of the hotel's guests were using the upper floors as a place to entertain their customers with beautiful women whom they furnished with the rooms. Our hotel made the local papers and we all had a laugh over it. I remember I had placed a chair up against my door just in case any of the gorgeous, well-shaped women tried to get into my room. (I put the chair on the outside.) I also thought about Kruger Park. I would love to see it sometime in the future when the trees are green with leaves and when the animal population has increased. It had been interesting to see South Africa but the only reason I would ever want to go there again would be to see Kruger Park.

I also mused about the terrible fright I had in my room at the President Hotel. While I was roaming about the room late one night, lighting my way with my flashlight, all of a sudden a tough-looking character appeared directly in front of me. He looked very mean and I almost collided with him. I quickly sprung back in fear. Then I discovered that the mean-looking character was only my reflection in a mirror on one of the walls. It sure frightened the heck out of me. I told one of the tour members about it the next day and he laughed and said the same thing had happened to him!

In just a little while, we will be in Bulawayo, Rhodesia, then on to Zambia, our home for the next few days. The very name sounds exciting. I hope it will be full of wild animals and jungles.

4.   Victoria Falls_Zambia—Livingstone

Our next stop is to be Victoria Falls and the rain forest. Then on to Zambia. We were instructed by Steve to wear a raincoat and old clothes at the falls and to carry our cameras in a plastic bag because of the constant mist.

Our flight from Jo-Burg to Bulawayo in Rhodesia lasted about an hour. There we had a two-hour wait for the plane to Victoria Falls, a four-engine prop-jet. Even though it was only a 50-minute flight the stewardess served us a light lunch of sliced turkey, ham, salad, boiled eggs, rolls, and pudding. When landing I had hoped that the pilot would fly over the falls so we could see it from the air. It would have only taken a few minutes. The airport at Victoria Falls was in the midst of a wild veldt area that surrounded the airport on all sides. Still, as in Kruger, we were in the dry season and the trees were mostly bare. We made a smooth landing and shortly afterwards boarded a bus for a ride to the falls and rain forest.

Our guide was a pretty Irish girl named Jeanette Helen, who had a charming personality and a cute dimple on each cheek. I asked her where she got the dimples and she said from her Irish father. She pointed out things of interest to us as the bus rolled along on the way to the falls. We came to an enormous Baobab tree, which was one of the largest in the country, measuring 67 feet in circumference and 120 feet tall—a colossal structure! We all got out of the bus to examine it up close and to photograph it. The outside temperature was a hot 97 degrees. We were truly in the tropics now! Jeanette told us that next month the temperature would go as high at 130 and that we were lucky to be visiting the country during the "cool" weather. Although it was boiling hot, the air was bone dry with practically no humidity. All about us was pretty wooded veldt in a semi-arid condition. I couldn't picture us needing raincoats or overshoes in just a few minutes as we had been instructed by Steve. But sure enough, as we drove on a short distance, and when the bus stopped, we could hear a tremendous roar from the falls ahead. In a matter of minutes we

were following our pretty guide down a wooded path toward the falls. The air was still bone dry and the trees lifeless and dusty. Suddenly we were met by a chill breeze and then, right in front of us, magnificent Victoria Falls! The view was positively breathtaking and the roar was deafening. I looked at it in awe and then began taking pictures from every angle with all three of my cameras. I remembered my son Paul had stressed that I should take lots of pictures of the falls. The group had moved on and I was by myself. Steve finally came back and asked that I come along to catch up with the rest. He pointed out the dangerous slippery grass edge that dropped straight off to the boiling water far below. One slip would mean certain death. I told him I wanted to photograph the falls and he laughed.

"This isn't all of it," he yelled above the roar of the falls. "This is only a tiny part of it. The falls goes on for a whole mile, all the way to the Zambesi border." I followed him almost in disbelief. I thought I was looking at the whole falls at that one spot. Then as I walked along the path through the rain forest, a dense mist filled the air, making it necessary for me to stop and put on my raincoat. I had to cover my camera with a plastic bag as we had been advised beforehand. Then I saw more of the falls in every direction, huge cascades of water pouring over the edge of a high cliff and beautiful rainbows arching over the churning waters. It was fantastic. I told Steve that this was absolutely the highlight of the whole trip, and I think he agreed. Every turn of the path brought us to a new lookout and a different view of the falls. It looked like there were miles of falls—some massive and huge, others filmy and wispy-looking, almost like smoke floating through the air. The rainbows, which are always there, even show up in photographs.

In some areas the mist was so heavy it came down like sheets of rain. Without our raincoats we would have been soaking wet. I would uncover just the lens as I took pictures to avoid wetting the entire camera, which could damage its mechanism. Once in a while

On the way to Victoria Falls we stopped to look at a huge Baobab tree, the largest in Rhodesia. It is 67 feet in circumference.

I would have to wipe the spray from the lens as it became covered with water and fog very quickly. The rocks and grassy edge of the walkway near the falls were wet and very slippery. There were no restraining ropes of any kind and the only thing that separated you from a sheer drop of several hundred feet was a growth of grass. If you didn't know there was a cliff there you could easily walk off to your death, especially at night. The walk along the falls went on for about a half mile along a beautiful pathway through a dense rain forest of tall, tropical trees. It looked like a real jungle. But the "rain" for the forest comes not from the sky but from the constant mist of the falls. Each stop presented a spectacular view of the falls as we followed the path all the way to the Zambesi border. The Zambesi River separates the two countries. We walked out to a sheer cliff and our guide, Jeanette, pointed out the fantastic view below that is almost unbelievable. It is called the "boiling pot" where the water from the falls spins and twists into a most violent upheaval of totally wild water. It looks like a caldron of boiling water.

"Pretty spectacular, isn't it," Jeanette said to me. I agreed. Then after taking pictures of it, I asked Jeanette if she would like to have her picture taken by the falls. She was delighted. She said no one had ever taken one before, and I promised to mail them to her. Then she told me that I should walk down to the bridge as long as I was this far along the trail and they would hold the bus for me.

I had stopped along the trail to photograph a family of wart hogs that were feeding along the edge of the forest. I was able to walk right up to them and took some good movies. Steve came running. He thought they might attack me. Then I walked down to the bridge for a quick look and finally headed back to the bus, stopping along the way for a last look at mighty Victoria Falls at each place that seemed interesting. I was so impressed by the falls that I would say it is worth a trip to Africa just to see it. It is one of the wonders of the world! I was so impressed with it that I ran back for one more look at the "boiling pot," one of the most spectacular sights of all. It looks as if the earth simply split open at one time and the entire mile-wide Zambesi River poured over the edge into the crack. This is probably how it was formed.

We all returned to the bus and in minutes we were out of the area, back in the bone-dry country with its 97-degree temperature. Incredibly it had been almost cold at the falls. We drove a very short way and then had to change buses, for our bus with Jeanette couldn't leave Rhodesia. The next bus was very small and I

Victoria Falls, which go on for nearly a mile, present a spectacular view. This was our first look at it.

Against the spraying mist of the falls you might be able to pick out a double rainbow.

didn't think we could all fit. But they turned down jumpseats in the aisle and crowded us in like sardines. Not only were we extremely crowded, hot, and uncomfortable, but we had our hand luggage in our laps as well. As we left Victoria Falls I said goodbye to Jeanette. We were off for Zambia!

In just a few minutes we crossed the bridge over the Zambesi River and were in Zambia, where we had a sticky problem with immigration. We all had to fill out two sets of papers with the usual, surname, passport number, length of stay, proposed address, etc. Checking papers and passports took over two hours and included a fee of $3.15 for visas. This wasn't cov-

ered in our original tour for some reason. It was now night time and we boarded the crowded bus for the trip to the Musi-O-Tunya hotel—only a few minutes drive. Musi-O-Tunya means, "the smoke that thunders" in native language. The early natives of the country had told Dr. Livingstone of the strange smoke that thundered when they led him to the falls.

The hotel was fabulous. Once again I must compliment Percival Tours on their excellent selection. Very modern with a beautiful swimming pool, Musi-O-Tunya was set right in the center of the African Veldt with woods all around it. The air-conditioned rooms were neat and decorative. After dropping off our hand luggage in our rooms, we all sat down for dinner. Several waiters quickly tended to us with instant service and friendly smiles. The sign at the entrance to Zambia had said it was a friendly country and it certainly is. Everyone there was exceptionally nice to us. Everyone was very thirsty after the hot bus ride and we were soon flooded with water. Back in Jo-Burg we usually had difficulty getting a drink of water in both the hotel and the game lodges, but here you were brought all you wanted with a smile. It was delicious water, crystal clear and tasty. We had been advised not to drink water at every place along the route, but I figured that with 75 million gallons of water pouring over

the falls every minute, just 900 feet away, surely the water must be fit to drink. When you are very thirsty you are less likely to be selective about water, and nearly everyone drank it. But later we learned that the water here was both filtered and sterilized, which of course made it perfectly safe to drink. For dinner I had lamb chops, fried potatoes, salad, and dessert. Then went out and sat by the pool with a couple of the guests. It was pleasant at night—the air was slightly cool and refreshing. In the distance you could hear the roar of the falls. Every now and then when the wind would blow from the right direction, you could feel a chill as the cool air from the falls was swept inland.

Main Falls, one of the most spectacular sights at Victoria Falls. Note tiny human figures at top right. The falls go on for nearly a mile. A foot path takes you along the edge of the precipice. Each view is more breathtaking than the last.

This magnificent view of the falls was taken from the bridge that connects two countries—Rhodesia and Zambia.

My room was on the first floor of the hotel and I could look out at the swimming pool. The airconditioner kept the room very comfortable; however those who stayed on the second floor said their rooms were very hot. Apparently the boiling sun with its near 100-degree temperature would beat down on the roof all day and would heat up the room in spite of the airconditioner. Most of them changed to a downstairs room the next day. I washed more of my clothes and hung them up in the bathroom. We would be here for three days so it was a good opportunity to catch up on my laundry. Then I went to bed for a much needed sleep after a long day. The bed was very comfortable (there were twin beds in the room) and a large carved wooden mask hung on each wall. Huge floor-to-ceiling windows overlooked the pool. I fell asleep happy and contented.

Tuesday, Sept. 30

After a hearty breakfast of orange juice, toast, bacon and eggs, sliced fresh pineapple, ham, and coffee, we boarded tour buses to visit the town of Livingstone. We used two buses so we wouldn't be too crowded. We had enough of that crowded bus the night before.

The town of Livingstone, Zambia. Notice how clean and uncrowded it is.

An example of primitive art from Zambia.

Colorful masks from Zambia.

Livingstone, a small town with about one main street, was only a short drive from the hotel. We parked the bus and then walked around, mostly on our own, so we could shop and visit in the various stores. We came to a most interesting native curio shop with a huge selection of native wood carvings of every description. They had everything—shields, drums, masks, spears, beans, tools, etc.—and nearly everyone bought souvenirs. I bought several carved wooden masks of unusual design, some wooden knives, a strange musical instru-

ment used by the natives, a large ebony elephant that weighed about 18 pounds, and a strange witch doctor mask with a grotesque face and long hair. I thought Paul would like that. The last two items I had mailed from the gift shop as they were too heavy and bulky to carry with me for the rest of the trip. After I was given a receipt for them, and assured that they would be packed well and reach the States all right, I took all of the smaller items with me in a small shopping bag. I didn't know how I would carry them on the plane but I would worry about that later. I can always buy another suitcase if I get loaded down with enough souvenirs.

I had purchased the items mostly with American money, as all the shops would accept American dollars. I had a small amount of Zambian money with me that I was saving for inexpensive items. The black ebony elephant was a thing of real beauty. They also had spectacular carved rhino of the same material, but these were all bought out before I could get one. I thought I would be able to find a carved rhino somewhere else on the trip but I didn't see another like it anywhere. The elephant cost 10 Kwacha, more or less, which included postage to the U.S., and the rhino was similar in price. One Kwacha K1.00 is $1.40, which is the same as the Rand in South Africa. The Kwacha is divided into smaller denominations of 100 ngwee, and it doesn't take long to figure out its approximate value as compared to American money.

After shopping we went to the Livingstone Museum,

The back side of witch doctor mask is intricate rope netting so that it can be placed over the head.

A strange musical instrument is one of my prized souvenirs of the safari. Each time I strum it, it brings back memories of Africa. I got it in Zambia.

an interesting place with fine displays of native artifacts, culture, old elephant guns, and many items that were in use in the early days of Dr. Livingstone. Across the street we visited the tourist office and were given a large, colorful, Zambia travel guide, which tells all about the country and is illustrated with many beautiful photographs of animals in the many game preserves here. There is also a superb color shot of Victoria Falls in the book. I would certainly recommend that anyone planning a trip to Zambia should write to the Zambia National Tourist Bureau, Mosi-oa-Tunya Road, Livingstone, Zambia, for a copy so you can see all the country has to offer. The huge game preserves, where you see the game *on foot,* sound *very* interesting.

It was now nearly lunch time so we returned to the hotel where I ate with the usual crew: Trudy Kemeny, John Barbie, and Rose Meinhardt. We had a very pleasant time together and, as always, the lunch

A carved wooden mask from Zambia. We found the most interesting native curio shop in downtown Livingstone with carvings and native handicraft of every description.

A strange witch doctor mask that I found in a curio shop in Livingstone, Zambia.

was excellent, although this time I must admit, most unusual. I had no idea what it was but I decided to try *Nshima,* the national dish of Zambia. I was a little shocked when I got it. On the menu it said that it was a combination of mealy-meal and tender beef tips. But the mealy-meal (ground white corn mush) was heaped up in my plate into a large white ball, which looked like a huge brain. But then I got the dish of beef and gravy and poured this over the white mass.

It was surprisingly tasty but extremely filling and I could only eat about a fourth of it. It was pleasant to sit in the air-conditioned dining room for the outside temperature was oppressive. I marveled at how luxuriously we were able to see and enjoy the wonders of Victoria Falls and the mysterious tropics compared to the early explorers who slept in tents and fought disease and hostile natives in this very area. Here we enjoyed it all in the utmost of comfort.

Wooden knife and black ebony letter openers from Livingstone.

I discovered these exotic carved birds at the gift shop by the Falls at Zambia.

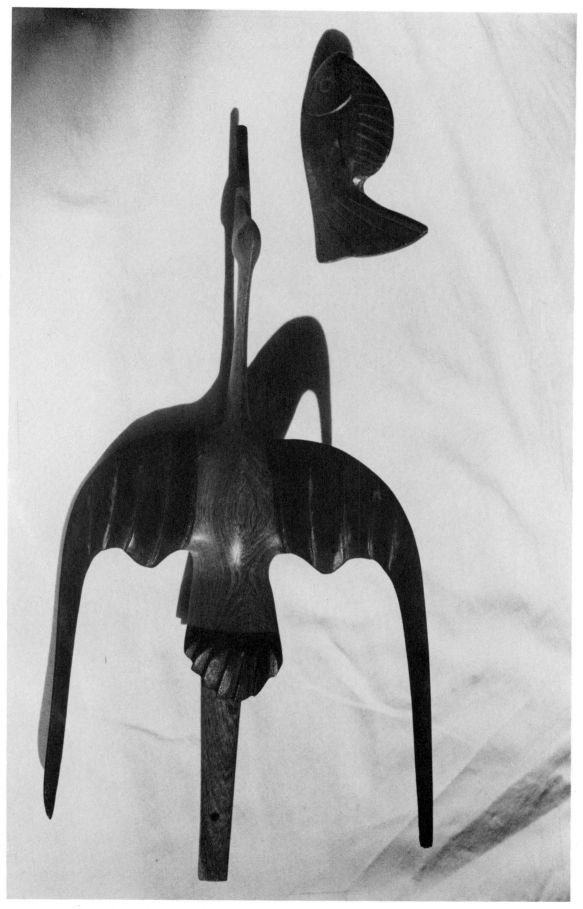

Beautiful carved bird from Zambia. It makes a handsome wall decoration.

At Zambia, we found a native gift shop down by the falls. I picked up these interesting carvings there.

I carried my cameras and flight bag with me to lunch as well as on all our day tours throughout the entire trip. My movie camera was kept in the flight bag and the other two cameras were carried over my shoulder. I carried a daily supply of film in the bag, a writing pad, glasses, plus my passport and some money. I also put all my exposed film in it so that each day it got a little heavier. I considered the film to be my most precious item—especially the exposed film—and didn't want to take a chance on it being lost or subjected to excess heat en route, so I simply carried it with me. Also I didn't want to leave my money, passport, or valuables in the hotel all day so I carried them also. It worked out just fine.

In the afternoon we visited the Livingstone Open Air Museum, an outdoor display of native huts from all parts of the country. Some of the natives did a dance for us. One of them got inside a strange, turtle-like object, which we were told was supposed to be a hyena. Another native beat out a tune on some drums while the "hyena" dancer swayed back and forth. There were supposed to be witch doctors here but we didn't see them. On the way to our next stop, the Livingstone Game Park, we rode the bus through a beautiful wooded area and along the banks of the Zambesi River. It was a pretty drive through wild, jungle-like, country. We saw signs of hippo along the road and were told that there were a number of them in the area. They are totally protected so they can build up in numbers. Although the game park is small, occupying only two square miles, it was an interesting place. It was like Kruger on a small scale.

The Livingstone Open Air Museum has a large collection of native huts from all over the country.

We visited the famous Livingstone Museum in Zambia. It presented an early history of the country.

A chief's hut in the Open Air Museum at Livingstone.

The first animals we saw there were two huge white rhinos that had been imported from South Africa. We were told that they were trying to re-establish them in Zambia as a conservation measure. We were able to get quite close for pictures of these animals that looked like something out of the past. We toured the park in small mini-buses, like those we used in Kruger. Soon we came across a small herd of beautiful water buck, then zebras. We could get very close to them as they were almost tame and well accustomed to cars and buses. One zebra came over to the bus, stuck his head in the window, and let us pet him. One time he got in front of the bus and he would push his body against the bus in an effort to keep us from moving. The driver finally had to build up power in the vehicle and push him out of the way. We all got good pictures of both zebra and waterbuck.

Then we came across a good-sized herd of impala, which were also very tame, hardly moving out of our way. We also saw buffalo, a huge sable antelope, baboons, wart hogs, guinea fowl, and giraffe. The giraffe were of unusual color and a rare species known as the Thornicroft Giraffe. We saw many wart hogs and several large monitor lizards that would dart across the road in front of us. Even though the park is only two square miles, we spent about three hours in it, driving back and forth along the winding roads. We never saw any fences and it looked like we were in a savage wilderness. I thought to myself that this is exactly how a zoo should be—not a steel and concrete jail cell for the animals like it is in many. Here is an ideal zoo, where the animals are free to roam about in a natural, protected area. There is a fence around it to keep the animals in and unwanted animals and

A native hut at the Open Air Museum in Livingstone, Zambia. There were a representative group of native huts in the compound and we could walk through them for study at close range.

The Livingstone Game Park is a section of forest and veldt surrounded by a fence to keep the animals in the area. It encompasses several square miles. We took an interesting afternoon drive through the area. Once we passed through the gate, we didn't see the fence again until we left the park. A young buffalo is guarding the entrance.

Many of the animals in the Livingstone Game Park are tame. Here a zebra visits our minibus.

Buffalo at Livingstone Game Park. Note the bird perched on its nose.

White rhino mother and calf. The white rhinos are much larger than the black rhino but have a gentler disposition. They are found only in the Livingstone Game Park in Zambia but eventually will be reintroduced to other areas. We saw these interesting beasts right at the entrance to the park. (Photo courtesy Zambia National Tourist Bureau.)

A white rhino with its calf at the park. The huge beasts were imported from South Africa in an attempt to establish them in Zambia. The white rhino is the world's second largest animal, the elephant ranking number one.

A small herd of impala at Livingstone Game Park. The preserve is simply a wooded area with a fence around it yet it harbors an immense quantity of game with no bars or cages. This is the ideal "Zoo." The animals live in a beautiful natural area and you view them by simply driving through in a mini-bus or land rover. We could use a number of animal parks like this in our own country.

A colorful crowned crane in the park.

Rare Thornicroft Giraffe has subdued coloring and blends into the foliage. A number of them live in the protection of the game park.

A young bushbuck beside the road at Livingstone Game Park.

people out, but it is hidden from view by trees and the winding road. It is simply a matter of selecting a natural site, then putting a good fence around it. Your zoo is all finished! You don't need any zoo keepers, cage cleaners, or attendants. No one except an occasional guard to keep poachers out. This is the kind of zoo I would like to build in America, some place in the Southern part of the country, and it could be done. I would like to build it on 50 square miles and make it as wild and authentic as the African jungle. All I would need is the land and a good fence. Then I could bring over giraffe, impala, zebra, rhinos, hippos, and all the animals. Some day, if I can get the financing or if I ever get rich from one of my books, I would like to do it. I worked on such a project for nearly five years at one time, working out every detail. I even had the land for it but never quite got it going.

I was very pleased with the Livingstone Game Park. I was told that they intend to enlarge it substantially, which also made me happy. I told our driver that I would like to see a lot more animals the next time I come to Zambia. I told him that the reason I came to Africa was to see the wild animals—its greatest tourist attraction. I am sure they realize it, judging from the keen interest in game preserves that is apparent throughout the continent. The little park boasts five white rhinos, several giraffe, and perhaps several hundred antelope and buffalo. The trees and grounds in the park were typical veldt and very scenic for photography.

On our way back to the hotel, the road was covered with hippo dung in some areas, giving evidence that the huge beasts were about. They usually come out of the water only at night to feed on the lush grasses along the banks of the river. Sometimes they walk far inland in search of succulent grasses or even native crops, and it can be dangerous to come across one after dark. They kill a certain number of people every year and are considered the most dangerous animal on the continent by many naturalists.

We arrived back at the hotel in the early evening, just in time to watch a spectacular African sunset. I didn't use the pool at all. Being a skin diver I had enough of swimming for a while. However, I did note some exotic women in very small bikinis cavorting

about and found them nearly as fascinating to watch as the wild game (perhaps even more so).

As the sun retired, I did likewise to my room to freshen up for the pool-side barbecue, to which all guests were invited. The barbecue dinner was especially nice. There was a huge array of food: baked potatoes, shish-kebab, sausage, a whole roast lamb, and a whole suckling pig. Then there was native music with drums and a xylophone. The whole setting beside the pool—the cool tropical night under a billion stars—combined with the luscious dinner and the music was

A small herd of waterbuck in the game park. This is an ideal way to protect and preserve animals. It's like a large zoo except that it doesn't require any zoo keepers or cage cleaners, making it far superior to the old zoos of steel and concrete. This method should be adopted in America. It's simply a matter of fencing off a wooded area. You view the animals by driving through in a minibus or land rover.

We found this interesting gift shop near the falls in Zambia. It was just a few minutes' walk from the hotel. One of our tour members bargains with them for a gift.

an unforgettable occasion and a pure delight. I could hardly believe that all this was happening to me. Despite the torrid heat of the day, evenings out-of-doors were surprisingly pleasant. I noticed not a single mosquito. As I partook of the delicacies, which by the way included hush puppies and barbecued chicken, I could hear the distant roar of Victoria Falls during a lull in the music. I could feel an occasional chill as a draft of air directly from the falls passed over us as if to freshen the already pure air.

Tomorrow, as an extra activity not included in the regular tour, about half of the group will fly over the

falls in a small plane. It will cost us $6 each for the trip. We will fly over the falls and then across Wankie Park to see wild game from the air. I am looking forward to it very much. I mulled over these thoughts as I retired for the evening. I found out why my wrinkle-proof, drip-dry shirts looked like one giant wrinkle when they dried. You aren't supposed to wring them out! You are supposed to hang them up wet and let the water drip out of them. I resoaked the clothes and even washed out a pair of drip-dry slacks, hanging them up the proper way. This time they looked great when they dried. I didn't have to wear a coat or tie at

Crude but interesting, this carving was purchased from a native gift market just a few minutes' walk from our hotel in Zambia.

Wooden knife, back scratcher, native axe from Zambia.

all in Zambia. The hotel is strictly informal and you can wear anything you like. This suited me fine.

Wednesday, Oct. 1

After a hearty breakfast I was ready for the new day that was to be full of all kinds of projects. First we boarded a bus for a short, two-minute ride to the falls, where we would see them from a new bridge that had just been opened. We walked down a beautiful wooded path and this time we would see the falls from the Zambesi side. Our first view was a beautiful rainbow arching over the woods. As we approached the Mist Forest we were handed raincoats, which had been provided by the hotel. We soon came to the new bridge that went across a deep gorge, and far below were tremendous forests, mostly of palms. The mist here came down in torrents, almost like water coming out of the spray nozzle of a garden hose. The view of the falls was much the same as on the Rhodesia side, equally breathtaking. The new bridge allowed people to walk all the way along the falls to the Rhodesian border. The bright sunny day highlighted the white foam of the falls as we walked through the beautiful "Mist forest" along a new path that was being constructed along the way. Finally we came to the very end of the falls where they tumble into the Zambesi river far below. This was the most spectacular view. Far across the deep chasm were the cliffs on the Rhodesian side where we had stood just two days before looking across into Zambia. I saw a small group of people on the cliff and wondered if our guide Jeanette was there with them, but it was too far away to identify anyone. I took many photos, uncovering my camera from beneath my raincoat each time I wanted to take a picture. There was a strong breeze blowing today and it whipped the spray about even more than usual. Some of the older women had decided not to walk all the way down to the end of the walk, which I think was wise as it was extremely wet and slippery. I never tired of looking at the majestic beauty of the falls.

We returned to the hotel to drop off those who were not going on the plane ride. They would go into Livingstone to shop instead. Then we drove to the Rhodesian border, where the usual formalities with immigration and customs were conducted. We had to present our passports and pay 30¢ in Zambia money to have the passport stamped so we could leave. Next, we drove another few minutes and had to stop at Rhodesia's immigration office, where we had to fill out immigration forms again and present passports. I thought it was ridiculous that such paperwork was

necessary just to go back into Rhodesia for a couple of hours. It took nearly an hour just to clear customs and immigration for both countries. Finally, we went out to a tiny airport for our flight over the falls.

The planes were small Cessnas and we took off shortly after our arrival. The flight, which lasted less than 15 minutes, was disappointing. The planes were much too fast to properly view or photograph the falls from the air. We were over the falls in minutes and the plane buffeted around very badly making picture taking almost impossible. Also we did not get down close. It was much more spectacular from the ground. We circled the falls a couple of times, each time so fast that it was very difficult to even get the camera aimed because of the acrobats of the plane. Then we flew along the Zambesi River, but very high. We saw a small herd of hippo, which looked like tiny dots from our altitude, and a couple of elephants. The pilot flew down close to them but he flew so fast and with such a tight, swirling maneuver that I could hardly take more than a few frames of movie film of the beasts. I even got a little sick from the tight turns. I did get a chance to see a little of Rhodesia from the air. I happily noted that unlike South Africa, which is all developed, both Rhodesia and Zambia still have large areas of veldt and jungle. Man has already destroyed enough of his world. It is time we protect what little wild area is left.

A few minutes later the plane landed quickly and we were driven back to the Victoria Falls Hotel. I didn't consider the short 15 minute flight worth it at all. I had thought we would fly over Wankie Game Preserve and see a great many animals. I found out later that the flight over the Game Preserve was a different flight and cost about $35. Even then I personally don't think it would be worthwhile in those fast planes. We had to wait for another bus to take us into Zambia. I purchased some interesting booklets on animals and birds of Rhodesia, also a magazine about the country. In addition I obtained some free pamphlets. While in Rhodesia I was able to mail my postcards of the falls. I had purchased Rhodesian stamps a few days before and was told that I couldn't mail the cards with the Rhodesian stamps from Zambia. Which reminds me, on a tour such as this, where you travel from one country to the next in a matter of days, always make certain that you mail your cards and letters *in the country where you get the stamps.* Also spend all your money before you leave, as it is usually no good in the next country.

The bus finally came and it dropped us off by a large tree, some distance from the border. We had to walk all the way from Rhodesia to Zambia—about two

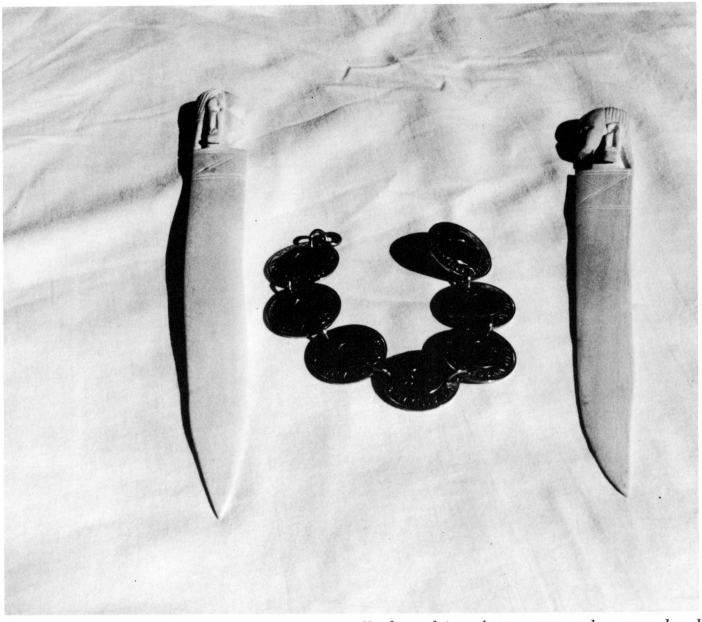

Hand-carved ivory letter openers and a copper bracelet from Rhodesia.

miles—in the heat. I didn't mind it at all though as it gave me a good chance to see the countryside. Finally we came to the bridge over the Zambesi River. The Zambesi border is right in the center of it, where you get a magnificent view of the falls, perhaps the best view of all, for it shows both the falls and the churning Zambesi River below. I took more photos, both movies and stills. The rest of the group was far ahead. I don't know what the hurry was as I didn't see what

difference a few minutes could make so far as affecting our itinerary for the day. I finally caught up with them and we all went through customs together. It didn't take as long this time and we were soon back at the hotel. I was nearly dying of thirst and drank a whole pitcher of ice water.

It was now lunch time. I sat with Mr. and Mrs. Perry Pierce from Springfield, Illinois. Perry was the life of the party, pleasantly greeting everyone with a loud welcome. His charming wife was equally nice. We all varied our orders as much as possible so that we could try just about everything on the menu. If it looked especially good when it was brought to the table, we would often tell the waiter to bring the same for everyone. This always pleased them for, because of the language barrier, it was easier for them to remember one dish rather than try to take a complicated order.

The natives around both Rhodesia and Zambia were very friendly and polite, and most could speak a few words of English. They seemed very happy, always ready to crack a smile or laugh at a little joke. One evening when my waiter had brought me a broiled lamb chop dinner, he was just about to serve it when I looked up and exclaimed,

"That doesn't look like scrambled eggs to me!"

The waiter lifted his head in surprise and didn't quite know what to do. Then I told him it was just a joke and he roared with laughter. All around the hotel they waited on us hand and foot, opening doors and bringing us anything we wanted. If you said, "thank you" for some little favor they would say "thank you" in return. I never saw any hostility in their eyes because we were white, anywhere on the entire continent.

I walked down to the falls to visit a native gift market and found that prices here were about a fourth what they were in Livingstone. There was also a wider selection. I purchased some beautiful carved birds, more masks, and a few little odds and ends, wondering how in the world I would be able to fit them in my one suitcase and already over-stuffed flight bag. I noted with horror that engineers were building a hydro-electric plant right next to the hotel, digging a huge trench that will carry water from above the falls to generate electricity. I was told that when the gates are opened to the trench, the flow of water over the falls will be reduced and some of the smaller falls will cease to flow, particularly in the dry season. What a crime! To destroy a natural wonder just for electricity seems tragic. Why can't an atomic power plant be used instead of slowly destroying this magnificent wonder. I understand the same thing is being planned at Murchison Falls, right in the center of one of the greatest game preserves in all the world. How can a country do this? Don't they realize that tourism brings millions of dollars and that Victoria Falls, Murchison Falls, and the wildlife are the *only* things that tourists come to see. If these are destroyed or badly marred, they will lose the tourist dollars. Then they won't need the electricity. I think they should find some other source of electricity other than Victoria Falls. It is entirely fea-

sible to use atomic power in this modern age and the money brought in by tourism would pay for such a plant, rather than destroy a natural world wonder with power lines and turbines. I hope no more plants are built at Victoria Falls. It is developed more than enough so far as I am concerned.

Our next event of the day will be a ride up the Zambesi River in the "Zambesi Queen," a large motor launch. I was photographing a bikini-clad female at the pool when I noted that our bus had arrived to take us to the river. The young lady and her husband were living in Africa in a town called Chingola, Zambia. Ann and Allen Patterson were vacationing at the hotel for about a week. I told her I was writing a book about Africa and would like to put her picture in it. They were both thrilled about it but I couldn't promise that the picture would be used.

Then I boarded the bus with the other members of the tour and we headed for the Zambesi River along a road that went through a dense wooded forest. Finally we came to the river and the boat was tied up in a quiet cove surrounded by floating plants and huge trees all along the bank. It looked like a real jungle river and I was thrilled at the prospect of the ride. As we boarded the boat I noted that there were many empty seats, most likely a quiet and peaceful cruise. We were just about to cast off when two buses drove up loaded with Indian children and their mothers who began piling aboard until every seat was filled. Our peace was over. There is no such thing as a quiet youngster, and Indian children are no exceptions. I soon had an entire family crowded into my seat: the mother, a small boy with jet black eyes, a cute little girl about three years old, and an older girl about nine.

Cruise boats along the Zambesi River.

*A jungle area along the Zambesi River. We started on our
ride up the Zambesi from this beautiful tropical area.*

They were very polite and well behaved and smiled at me with their shiny dark eyes. As the mother spoke to them from time to time, I gradually learned their names. I would call them by name, which would bring on more smiles. Then I took out some hard candy and passed it out among them, giving the mother some also. The mother was dressed in a pretty sari, the usual Indian dress and she had a bright red dot painted in the center of her forehead. When I asked the young girl her name she replied, "Aleta." I thought I was making good progress, considering the language barrier, when the lady in front of me, who was with our tour, turned and asked the girl's mother a question. Then Aleta spoke in perfect English and told her that her mother didn't understand English. I was shocked to hear that she spoke our language and she said all the children did. We talked a little after that and she told me that her father was a merchant, operating a store in Livingstone. She was a very pretty little girl with beautiful dark brown eyes and hair. She also had a free, ready smile that is typical of most children. I broke out some chewing gum to strengthen the friendship.

The launch ride itself was somewhat of a disappointment. I was expecting to see all kinds of wildlife all along the banks of the river, but we saw practically none. We went for mile after mile and saw nothing. Finally we caught sight of a small herd of hippo but we did not get very close. I had to use the telephoto lens of my movie camera to photograph them. They splashed and yawned for us but we didn't approach them close enough for good pictures. We were told that if the boat got too close they would just submerge and we wouldn't be able to see them at all. The light was poor as it was 5:30 P.M. Perhaps if we had left earlier in the day, we would have been able to see them in bright sunlight. It was beautiful along the river, though, and there were many huge tropical trees mixed in with tall grasses. On the Rhodesian side the entire banks of the river for 35 miles have been made into a wildlife preserve. I wished that Zambia would do the same so that the river could be kept wild. It certainly would hold little lure to the tourist if cottages and outboards took over the scene.

As the boat cruised along the glassy smooth water, the children began to sing some pretty Indian songs. Now we had exotic music to enhance the voyage. Then all of a sudden we saw a large elephant right along the bank. The children all hushed so as not to frighten it. It was not facing us and the view it presented to the camera was not the most photogenic so I passed it up, hoping it would turn around. Instead the huge

beast walked along the banks in the dense grass, shaking the trees as it passed by them. The grass, which must have been 15 feet tall, largely hid the huge creature.

The boat moved on and the children began to sing again. Then another boat, completely filled with Indian children and their parents, came into view. They apparently were friends of the Indian people on our boat, for as soon as the boat pulled alongside of us the children began frantically waving and shouting at each other. The boat was soon tied up to us and then the two began drifting toward the shore. I thought we would run aground for certain. I assumed that the other boat needed assistance but I was wrong. The whole encounter was done simply to collect fares from the second boat. Apparently the money hadn't been collected at the dock and our boat Captain wanted to be sure to get it before the other returned. The boats finally parted when we were only about 30 feet from shore and we continued our cruise up the famous Zambesi.

We saw no more game, not a single hippo or even crocodile. I felt sad for this area should have been teeming with wildlife. Instead, it apparently had all been killed off. I wondered if it would make a comeback. Surely the tourist commission in Zambia wants the tourists to see wild game when they cruise up the wild Zambesi. I hope that the river is not developed into fishing camps and hotels. The lure of Africa is its jungles, elephant, hippo, giraffe and crocodile. We hadn't seen a single crocodile on the entire cruise!

I was disappointed with the river cruise. It was a pretty ride but I could take a pretty ride on any river in our own country. The cruise continued on until almost dusk, and since there was no wildlife to see I passed the time by chatting with my "adopted" family. I had moved the little girl over to the railing and held the little boy on my lap. The mother was all smiles at the attention I had paid to her family. I wondered what thoughts went on in the little heads of the children as they looked at us. The girl told me that she and the others learned English at a Catholic school in Livingstone.

We reached the dock just before dark, and then returned to the hotel for another superb meal. Steve told me that one time when he had cruised the river the whole bank was lined with elephants. I don't know whether he was joking or not but it was certainly possible as there is a game preserve on the Rhodesian side.

Tonight is our last night in Zambia. We didn't get a chance to see the falls lit up by floodlights as mentioned on the itinerary because the engineers were

THE SAFARI CAMP—KAFUE NATIONAL PARK: *Located many miles from the nearest habitation on the banks of Kafue River, where good fishing abounds. Guests at Ngoma Lodge can sleep in the bush on overnight trips as part of their stay at the Lodge for no extra charge. Camp staff prepare all meals and see that thatched huts are ready for the guests every night. (Photo courtesy Zambia National Tourist Bureau.)*

using all available electricity to work on their hydro-electric plant. But I don't think anyone really minded at all. We had seen the falls from all sides and I am sure everyone was more than satisfied. But of course it is impossible to please everyone. We had grumbles and complaints by some of the members of the group from time to time. There would also be slight problems in seating on the buses. Some people would object if you took a picture over their shoulder, but they thought it was all right when they took pictures over *your* shoulder. On a trip like this you have to give and take. You just can't take the best seat on the bus every time. In Kruger we rotated our seats and this worked fine to everyone's satisfaction. There were times when some members of the group would get hostile toward the others. I would finally speak up and tell them that we were all on the trip together to have an enjoyable time and we shouldn't have bad feelings. It was evident when we first started the tour that we did not have a 100 percent compatible group (some would not even get into the group photo), but we didn't have any serious problems. The little grumbling would have to be contributed to tiredness or the natural tendency of people to complain (including myself).

Tomorrow we leave for Kenya and the big game preserves!

A PORTFOLIO OF WILDLIFE FROM ZAMBIA, THE FRIENDLY COUNTRY

Pictures courtesy of the Zambia National Tourist Bureau, Lusaka, Zambia

Zambia offers many exciting safaris through its magnificent wilderness areas. It has two huge big-game preserves as well as numerous smaller parks. The Kafue National Park is said to be the largest game preserve in all of Africa. Its 8,650 square mile area is the home of tens of thousands of elephants, buffalo, rhino, and all the great beasts. Zambia features unique foot safaris where you actually view much of the game on foot rather than through the windows of a minibus. This doesn't mean that you have to travel through the jungles on foot. You are driven to the choice areas and then allowed to disembark where you may approach the animals on foot, protected of course by armed guides. It is a pleasant departure from the usual minibus and land rover safari where you are *never* allowed to set foot on the ground except at the rest camp. Those who would like to really see the wild jungles with a little adventure thrown in should certainly look into these safaris as they would give you a taste of Africa at its finest. Your local travel agent can make all the arrangements for you through the Zambia National Tourist Bureau, 150 East 58th St., New York.

A herd of stunning sable antelope in Zambia.

Wood ibis in a Zambia preserve.

Wood Ibis feeding in Zambia game preserve. (Photo courtesy Zambia National Tourist Bureau.)

Buffalo are one of the most prolific species of large game in Zambia. They tend to travel in huge herds, sometimes numbering over a thousand heads. The mature animal stands five feet at the withers and weighs up to 1,750 pounds.

Buffalo on the Musa loop, Ngoma area, in Kafue National Park. (Photo by S. T. Darke Courtesy Zambia National Tourist Bureau.)

In one of Zambia's preserves a fine lion is ready to charge.

A waterbuck pauses in the shade, with a small bird for company, in the Luangwa Valley Game Preserve.

Lioness at Luangwa Valley, Zambia. (Photo courtesy Zambia National Tourist Bureau.)

A giant tusker at Luangwa Valley. (Photo courtesy Zambia National Tourist Bureau.)

Hippo are most often found along the rivers in Zambia's national parks, either playing in the water or grazing on shore. Schools of hippo may contain over 300 animals. A very pugnacious group, hippo fight over territory and inflict severe injuries on each other.

Hippo at Kafue National Park.

Elephant in the Luangwa Valley.

A large black rhino from Zambia.

A herd of kudu poses for the photographer.

Fishing along a river in Zambia.

An elephant family passing through a forest of strange sausage trees in one of Zambia's game preserves.

Nearly every morning at sunrise, the elephants cross into the game reserve at this spot in the Luangwa river. It is estimated that there are about 20,000 elephants here in this area.

A lion on a wildebeest kill at one of Zambia's wild National parks. A huge flock of vultures waits in the background.

A spectacular male kudu at Luangwa National Park.

The famous foot safari in Luangwa Valley brings you closest to the real African bush.

Wildebeest in Zambia at the river.

Artist David Shepherd paints his subjects in the Luangwa Valley preserve.

Two tourists view a distant herd of Cape buffalo in the Luangwa Valley preserve. This is probably the only major game area in Africa that can offer visitors the chance to get so close to animals.

An interesting shot of a giraffe in Zambia.

A lion stops to drink at a waterhole.

5. Nairobi—Mt. Kenya—Kenya—Treetops

Thursday, Oct. 2

Today we leave the Musi-O-Tunya Hotel and the friendly country of Zambia. I don't see how my stay there could have been any nicer. I asked the young couple, Allan and Ann Patterson, if there were real native villages in Zambia and Rhodesia and they said there were lots of them—some just a few miles from our hotel. They said you could drive up any dirt road a few miles from Livingstone and you would find them. I would like to have visited some of these villages but I found out about it too late, as we would be leaving the area very shortly. However, those making the trip in the future could certainly inquire about it. I made another trip down to the gift shop by the falls, which was only about a three- or four-minute walk from the hotel, to pick up a few more small items. Then it was back to the hotel for packing. I had a difficult time getting all of my gifts packed into the one small suitcase. The flight bag was completely full so I finally started filling a large shopping bag with masks, wooden knives, the musical instrument, and other smaller items. By now it was time for our final lunch in the beautiful air-conditioned hotel dining room. The lunch was served in the usual efficient manner. I had fruit cocktail, broiled chicken, french fried potatoes, rolls, coffee and integrated ice cream (half chocolate and half vanilla).

I noticed a few policemen around the hotel and then learned that his excellency, the President of Zambia, Dr. K. D. Kaunda, would visit the hotel later in the day. After lunch we boarded the bus for a ride to the airport. We were all on board and set to go when it was learned that the other bus driver had driven off with both sets of keys, so we had to wait about 20 minutes for another bus. Finally we were on our way. The drive to the airport took about 20 minutes and it gave me a chance to see a little more of the country. At the airport I saw the same group of Indians who had been on the boat ride with us. I said hello to Aleta and her mother and took a few photos of them. While we were waiting for the plane, they sang more songs and did a ceremonial dance. Then we boarded the plane and it took off just 20 minutes after we had arrived at the airport. I sat beside an attractive German girl named Marla. She spoke little English and I spoke no German so our conversation was very limited. She did say that she was on a wildlife safari from Germany and she had seen many animals in Zambia, but I couldn't find out whether she saw them at the Livingstone Game Park or at one of the other preserves. She also said she visited native villages there.

The plane had native Zambian stewardesses. The smooth flight was in a three-engine jet of some foreign make, a Bac-1-11. In less than an hour we landed at Lusaki, where we had to change planes for Nairobi. The airport here was extremely hot with no airconditioning. There was not the slightest breeze and it was quite uncomfortable. We had about an hour wait and then boarded the plane for our next stop—Ndola. This again was a very short flight. We actually spent much more time on the ground in between flights than we did in the air, which is common with modern air travel. At Ndola, which is located on the border of Zambia and the Congo, we had to go through immigration and have our passports stamped. There was about an hour and a half delay before our next flight, and we finally left for Nairobi at 4:45 P.M. We now flew in a twin jet plane with Rolls Royce engines. The plane was very comfortable but the short flights were tiring, especially because of the extreme heat. Also, we had to get off the plane at each stop and walk into the terminal, carrying all our hand luggage with us. In some instances there would be a very long walk and it was *very* tiring to carry the over-stuffed flight bag, three cameras, and my new package of souvenirs. I consider myself in good physical shape and if it tired me that much I just don't know how the older folks could possibly do it as they too were loaded down with flight bag, cameras, and usually a large pocketbook besides. I would strongly recommend that anyone making this trip, or a trip like it, bring along one very large, strong suitcase, into which you can put all the souvenirs, and just have it checked along with the baggage instead of trying to carry items with you. You will find it very tiring all along the route to carry items into the plane.

We are on our way to Nairobi at last and expect to be there in a couple of hours. A sudden thought struck me. We had been on safari for 11 days now and I really had not seen a great many animals, nothing like the giant herds I had envisioned and read about in my many books on Africa. I had seen a fair amount of game at Kruger, but no lions. I had only seen a few elephants and hippo but none were up close enough to even photograph. Livingstone Game Park was nice, but it was really a zoo as the animals were inside of a small fenced area.

I was almost beginning to panic at the thought that nearly half of our safari was finished and I had seen so few animals. I read the guide book given us by the Zambia tourist bureau and saw that they had huge game preserves all over the country. One of them was only a hundred miles from Livingstone. It said there were 20,000 elephant in the preserve as well as lions, hippo, herds of thousands of buffalo, and other game. You go on safari *on foot* there, with an armed guard, who takes you right in among the animals. In fact, the Kafue National Park in Zambia is said to be the largest game preserve in all of Africa, encompassing 8,650 square miles. It has seven tourist camps and a large river that flows through it for a distance of 150 miles, keeping the area green and lush. The brochure on the park showed herds of buffalo, wildebeest, lions, and elephants. They even feature a seven-day wilderness tour where a small group of people go out into the jungles in a land rover with a native guide. You sleep in a sleeping bag in tents erected each night at a new camping site. This sounds fabulous for the explorer-naturalist and I shall look into it further. You go into the wild, uninhabited areas far from civilization much the same as did the early explorers, Stanley and Livingstone. You will read about it in the Zambia Travel Guide.

There were numerous other preserves mentioned in the book and the more I read the more frantic I became. I wanted to see animals, not plush hotels and cities. We were in Livingstone for three days, why couldn't we have gone to one of the preserves? I must write to Percival about this when I return. Today was largely a waste of time. We spent most of the day sitting either on a plane or in an airport. As soon as the planes took off, they flew so high that we couldn't see anything on the ground. However, we did see some large forests over the Congo. I wish that someone

Nairobi is a modern city with many interesting shops and buildings. This area was only two blocks from our hotel.

would speak to the airlines about this. After all, most of the people on the plane are tourists and tourists want to see the country, not clouds at 30,000 feet. Why couldn't the plane fly at four or five thousand feet at least for part of the time?

We arrived in Nairobi after dark and were met at the airport terminal by Mrs. Betty Leslie-Melville, our Percival director for Kenya and East Africa. She was very nice and welcomed us to Kenya. She gave us each a new itinerary for our trip in Kenya and Tanzania and also handed out our hotel room keys. We would be staying at the New Stanley Hotel and were quickly driven there by bus. The evening temperature was a

The famous New Stanley Hotel is located in the heart of Nairobi.

cool 67 degrees and we felt a bit chilly after the torrid heat of Zambia. Tomorrow we go to Treetops, we were told; the next day, Mt. Kenya Safari club. But first we must have a good night's rest, as everyone was quite tired from the long day. I gathered up my hand luggage and went up to my room.

As I opened the door and looked inside, I was a little shocked. We had been so accustomed to sheer luxury in both Jo-Burg and Zambia that this hotel looked rather primitive compared to the modern, brand new places we had just left. The room itself was comfortable but very small. The bathroom was of ancient vintage with old-fashioned tub and shower. The New Stanley is not *new*. I think it is quite old, perhaps 50 years or more. But it is a very famous hotel and practically everyone who has come to Africa on big game hunts or wildlife trips has stayed here.

It was almost 9:00 P.M. and the dining room was about to close, so we all rushed down to dinner. The dining room was very nice, not new but charming in its own way, with elephant tusks arching over the doors. The food was very good, although perhaps not quite as exotic as Zambia, but it was very well presented nevertheless.

After dinner we walked around to settle our meal and at the same time look in the windows and see the town. The hotel is located right in the very center of town and the shops are all about it. Because it was late everything was closed, but we enjoyed window-shopping. I was accompanied by Trudi, John, and Rose, the group with whom I had most of my meals. We then returned to our rooms. I didn't sleep very well. The hotel was extremely noisy and all night long I heard people walking about or loud voices. There would be rattling of doors and banging of pipes. It was one of the noisiest rooms I have ever slept in. I kept thinking someone was trying to open my door. Finally I got up and put a chair against the door. I don't know why I couldn't sleep. I attributed it to the very late dinner, also to the extremely noisy floor—the sixth floor. The other hotels had been absolutely quiet. I finally got to sleep at a very late hour.

Friday, Oct. 3

We were called at 7:00 A.M. and I went to breakfast in the main dining room. I had fresh pineapple, orange juice, bacon, eggs, toast, and coffee. They have a large spread of juices, fruits, and cereals so that you can select whatever you like. This is standard in many of the hotels throughout Africa. I began to like the New Stanley more as I became accustomed to it. To compare it with a brand new hotel is not fair for it has a

background and charm that grows on you. The service is very good and the food is excellent. Later I found that they have all types of rooms and some are as delightful as any you can expect. My first room had been a small one on the sixth floor but some of the rooms are very luxurious. If we had stayed at the New Stanley first instead of the fabulous President at Jo-Burg we would have appreciated it more, but as it was we were slightly spoiled.

The fact that I hadn't really seen much wildlife so far on the journey began to disturb me more and more for this was my sole purpose in coming to Africa. When it was announced that we would make a tour of Nairobi, I flatly announced that I did not want to do it. I said I would like to visit Nairobi National Park instead and would see it if I had to go there all by myself in a private car. I came to Africa for only *one* reason—to see the animals. I told this to Steve and he said I should have taken the exclusive animal tour that Percival also features. He was right. If I had to do it again, I would have taken the animal tour. I had expected to see animals all over Africa, from Dakar to Jo-Burg. I thought I would see them from the outskirts of Jo-Burg all the way to Kruger Park. Instead I saw mostly cow pastures and barb wire fences. I thought Africa would be all animals once I got out of the cities, but it isn't. The animals have been killed off everywhere except for the game preserves, just like they have in our own country, even worse in South Africa. I made up my mind that if I ever do take another tour to Africa (which I surely will) it will be a 100 percent animal tour, in which every day is spent in a game preserve.

After breakfast we boarded a small, zebra-striped minibus and headed for Treetops, which is a long way from Nairobi, about 110 miles, but it is a pretty drive. Our driver was John Ochieng, a native of Kenya. He was very nice and a superb driver in whom I had the utmost confidence. We drove northward, stopping at the Chania Falls where there was a small gift shop. After seeing Victoria Falls, the Chania Falls was like a goldfish fountain and I don't think anyone was impressed with it. We drove on through the Kenya countryside. There were small coffee groves set among native huts punctuated with banana trees all along the route. There were also tea plantations, pineapple groves, and sisal hemp groves with more of the picturesque straw huts on the hills and plateaus of Mt. Kenya. In fact nearly all of the land around Kenya is cultivated or fenced with barbed wire from Nairobi almost to the very doorstep of Treetops. I was a little disappointed in this as I again expected to see wild game once I had left the outskirts of the city. But I saw not a single animal along the way even though I scanned the hillside for game. I began to wonder if all the game had been killed off in Kenya as it had in South Africa. We saw some spectacular views of Mt. Kenya and we stopped occasionally to take pictures.

At noon, we arrived at the Outspan Hotel for lunch, a beautiful place with some of the prettiest flowers and shrubbery that I have seen anywhere. It is a color photographer's delight. We had a delicious lunch with some type of macaroni and cheese and all kinds of meats, salads, and vegetables. The desserts were spread out on a huge table where you could take as much and any kind you desired. They had English trifles, a delicious pudding with fresh cream that was an utter ruination to anyone's diet.

I met two young girls from New York, Pat Zanelli and Aida Arroyo, who were on safari with a different tour. They had gone to Africa on their own and picked up a tour from Nairobi or Entebbe. They had been to Murchison Falls and said they saw so many animals you could hardly believe it. I told them I had seen practically nothing and I became more convinced that I should have taken the pure wildlife tour since my primary interest was animals.

After lunch we boarded land rovers for the final trip to Treetops. I watched in disappointment as we passed cornfields and barbed-wire fences. Is the whole world cultivated and civilized, I thought? Aren't there any more wild areas? The barbed-wire fences and gardens continued right to the very gates of the Aberdare National Park. I was a little disappointed in this for I think that the land rover ride to Treetops could be

On our way to Treetops we stopped at the Outspan Hotel for lunch. Here we exchanged our minibus for a land rover for the climb into the mountains.

greatly enhanced if they took a back road through wild area within the park so that you would see some game on your approach to the hotel instead of going right through the center of this civilized area.

Treetops is located in the Aberdare National Park, which has a total area of 228 square miles (they should enlarge it to 2,000 square miles before all the area is turned into gardens). It is a densely forested park with beautiful, snow-covered Mt. Kenya visible throughout most of the area. It has a population of several thousand elephant, buffalo, rhino, leopard, wart hogs, forest hogs, baboons, and antelope—including the rare bongo, one of the most beautiful of all antelopes. There is also a new forest-lodge in the park called the Aberdare country club and another called the Ark, which is said to rival Treetops in fascination and wildlife. One place, called the Secret Valley Lodge, specializes in leopards and you can see the elusive cats here on a regular basis.

It was just a short ride from the Outspan Hotel to Treetops. We arrived at our destination at 2:00 P.M. The land rover stopped at the foot of a path and we all disembarked. Then our guide, armed with a powerful rifle, led us to the huge treehouse. He told us that once we had climbed up into the lodge, we could not come down until morning as there were many dangerous animals about. Also he cautioned us about baboons, explaining that we must keep our windows closed when they visit the lodge, as they will steal or destroy anything they can get hold of, including cameras and equipment. He also requested that we keep our voices down so as not to frighten the animals away. Then we climbed up into the treehouse, which is about 40 feet above the ground, the house itself built around some large trees. We were assigned to our rooms and I had to bunk with two other men from our group. I put my flight bag and other gear on my bed, then grabbed a couple of cameras and went up to the roof to look around. At first, it didn't look like there would be anything around there. The "waterhole" where the animals are supposed to come to drink wasn't there at all. The rains had missed and the hole had dried up completely. But the area was said to contain a natural salt deposit and this was the main reason the animals were said to visit.

As soon as I got up to the roof I began to see animals, much to my surprise. I saw a great many wart hogs and numerous bushbuck that just stood around at the edge of the forest, often completely still like a statue. Then they would slowly and majestically walk right on down to the salt lick. There were about 60 people spending the night at the treehouse but it wasn't crowded at all since there are three floors to

Led by an armed ranger, our group heads for Treetops, the famous lodge built high among the trees. We spent a thrilling night there watching elephant, rhino, and buffalo cavort around a salt lick just 30 or 40 feet away.

this amazing place. I began taking pictures of the animals. This is an excellent place for photography, particularly for movies with a telephoto lens or still pictures with telephoto lens. You can take all the time you wish to compose your pictures and you can steady your camera on the railing of the treehouse for a high quality photo. There was a wonderful view of Mt. Kenya from the roof. I had to use my 300mm telephoto to bring the animals up close.

It was now about 5:00 P.M. and we all were waiting for the elephants to appear at any moment. Someone said they heard elephants trumpeting far off in the woods, but they didn't show up. More and more antelope and wart hogs came into view. There were bush bucks as well as other species of antelope. I photographed them with my 12-inch telephoto lens as well as with my movie camera. I could see as many as 50 animals at one time of various species. It was like a giant panorama of wildlife as animals would slowly emerge from the surrounding forests into the clearing. It was especially interesting to watch them with binoculars. They came so close you could hear their tongues scrape the hard ground for salt.

I really didn't expect to see any big animals here. There seemed to be nothing to attract them since the water hole had dried up, and the ground didn't look very salty. Pat and Aida were sitting on the roof with me. Treetops had also been included as part of their tour. They looked at the antelope and wart hogs for a while and then went off to bed. They had already seen thousands of animals before.

It was now growing quite late and sundown was

approaching. Suddenly a huge buffalo walked majestically out of the forest, followed by another, then another. They walked so quietly you could scarcely hear them. The first one, a big bull, would stop and sniff the air, then move on leading the others. They walked slowly and cautiously right up to the salt area and began licking the red ground with their rough tongues. You could hear them snorting as they approached other animals near the lick. They looked powerful, mean, and fully wild. They stopped about a 150 feet away and you could hear their coarse tongues scrape the ground and their heavy breathing. Because they moved so slowly it was easy to photograph them. They seemed to almost pose for pictures. The huge horns looked formidable. There were numerous other animals in the area so that you could easily photograph more than one kind in the same shot. I got some good close-up shots of the buffalo that nearly filled up the viewfinder on the camera.

I had just finished photographing the buffalo and was scanning the open area for more game when I saw two huge rhinoceros walk right out of the woods into the open. Like the buffalo, they were very cautious, stopping at short intervals to sniff the air. These were truly wild animals, not at all accustomed to people. When they approached a buffalo, they would stop and snort loudly at it. The buffalo would usually move out of the way. If I hadn't seen them walk into the area I would never have noticed them, for except for the occasional loud snorts they didn't make a sound despite their huge bulk. They slowly circled the open area and then walked back into the forest. I was able to take both movies and still photos of them even though they were only in the open for a few minutes. I used my 12-inch telephoto lens on the still camera and it brought them in just perfect for a picture. The light was very dim and I didn't know whether they would come out well at the time, but they did. I always take a chance with pictures if the subject is worthwhile. The most you can lose is a few frames of film, and sometimes very dramatic photos will result in the late evening sunset or during a deluge of rain.

I met a charming English lady who sat down beside me up on the roof. We watched the animals come and go until finally it grew dark. It also grew extremely cold so we went downstairs into the main lodge where it is much warmer. Here you can see the animals through large picture windows while sitting in comfortable lounge chairs. It is almost like sitting in a movie theatre. The animals are the actors who walk on and off the "stage" almost like clockwork. Powerful floodlights were turned on that lit up the entire area all the way out to the edge of the forest so that you could see everything in a large arena, several hundred feet across.

A number of buffalo were licking the salt when several rhino suddenly paraded into the scene. They would just suddenly appear out of nowhere, walking so quietly that you could not hear them at all, except for loud snorting whenever a buffalo did not move out of their way, or even when one of their own kind got too close. There was always a confrontation between the large animals whenever they met. They were always on the defensive and the buffalo would lower their massive heads in defiance whenever challenged by a rhino or by another buffalo. Occasionally two of the buffalo would fight, pushing and crashing together, but the fights were usually brief and soon everything would quiet down. The rhino would also rush at the buffalo if they didn't retreat immediately when they snorted at them, but the buffalo always gave way to the rhino when pursued. We now had about 25 buffalo and four rhino at the salt lick. All of a sudden someone exclaimed, "Elephant!"

Then just as silently as the buffalo and rhino had approached, ghost forms of elephant materialized in the darkness and swiftly paraded single file into view. They walked right into the center of the arena as if they owned the place, and both rhino and buffalo moved rapidly out of the way. There is no doubt that the elephant is the monarch of the jungle. The elephants kept coming—big, middle-sized, and baby elephants, scarcely three feet tall. It looked like they were mostly cow elephants with their young.

The mother elephants were extremely protective of their tiny babies and very touchy about anything coming near their precious little gems. One time a baby moved curiously toward a big buffalo and the mother let out a tremendous trumpet, charging at the buffalo and disrupting the entire scene. The buffalo scattered in all directions. The tiny baby ran under the legs of her mother for protection and gradually the area returned to normal. The elephants would constantly challenge the rhino by extending their trunks and moving toward them. The rhino would always back up and give way to them. The rhino in turn would do the same to the buffalo, making it move out of the way. It was a continuous show of authority. They would all stand quietly together licking the salt earth, each separated by a distance of ten feet or so. If an animal accidentally or intentionally got any closer there would be a loud snorting and a squaring off of the behemoths followed by a mock charge, the smaller animal usually retreating a few feet. Everyone watched the assembly of animals in utter fascination. The scene would constantly change as animals would disappear

From the roof of Treetops you get a magnificent view of the surrounding forest with snow topped Mt. Kenya as a background. Binoculars are useful here for you can spot all kinds of animals at the edge of the forest.

We sat on the roof to watch the animals. One by one they silently emerged from the forest. It was fascinating! A telephoto lens is a must here.

and silently reappear. It was almost as if someone had them all locked up in a huge barn and would turn them loose a few at a time to parade out into the circle of light. I asked our local ranger how many large animals were in the park. He said there were over 3,000 elephants, 6,000 buffalo, 400 black rhino, and thousands of others, including many forest antelope.

It was now 8:00 P.M. and dinner was announced. We all moved to the dining room—one large room that was big enough to accommodate 70 or 80 people at a time. This is rather amazing since the treehouse is built 40 feet above the ground. We were assigned seats with our name set at our place. A delicious soup was served, which felt good in the cool night air, and there was free wine, as much as you liked. Everyone came to dinner except the two young girls, Pat and Aida, who had gone to bed. They had colds and didn't feel well. We woke them up and they finally came down. They felt better after a hearty meal of roast duckling with orange sauce, rolls, salad, potatoes, cauliflower, and peas. For dessert brandy snaps and cream were served, followed with cheese and biscuits, as well as coffee. I told the girls about the elephants and we went downstairs to an outside viewing area where you are closest to the animals, about 20 feet above their heads. It was very cold outside and we were given blankets to wrap about us to keep warm. Then we sat back in comfortable chairs to watch the wildlife spectacle.

The scene was strange and ghostly. Everyone spoke in whispers so as not to frighten the animals. At times it would be utterly quiet. First there would be one or two elephants at the salt lick. Then a few more would wander in until the herd had increased to nearly 25. Four rhino stayed there most of the time and the buffalo varied from three or four to as many as 25 at a time. It was a weird, almost prehistoric scene, nothing like looking at animals in the bright sunlight. It was as though we had been transported back in time ten thousand years.

The elephants would get down on their knees and dig into the hard ground with their tusks to loosen the earth. Then they would reach into the hole they had made and pick up the loose earth with their trunk, squirting it into their mouth. They would chew it, sort of like taking snuff. The buffalo would lick the hard ground with their coarse tongues. The rhino would stick their horns into the ground with a quick thrust, then strain their heads backward until they had pried up a chunk of earth (like using a pick axe). Then they would pick up the loose earth in their mouths and chew on it. Sometimes they would dislodge a small rock and would chew on it for as long as a half

hour or more. You could hear heavy breathing, snorting, and the rasping tongue of buffalo licking the hard earth. The rest of the forest was totally quiet except for the occasional bark of a monkey (some monkeys make a barking noise almost like a dog) or the laugh of a hyena.

There was one half-grown elephant who would constantly disrupt the quiet scene much to the delight of the spectators. He must have been a boy, trying to show everyone how brave he was. He would charge at a nearby buffalo, trumpeting weakly and spreading out his ears in the typical charging position, but when the buffalo squared off to attack, the young elephant would immediately run back to his mother for protection. Everyone laughed at his "brave" behavior as he charged nearly every animal in sight, even the huge rhinos. But none of the animals were afraid of him. As soon as they would come after him, he would run behind his huge mother, who would then fend off the attacker with a menacing gesture of outstretched trunk and widespread ears. Nothing would dare stand up against the huge elephant. Even the rhinos backed off when challenged. The young elephant charged the other animals on and off all evening.

We also saw huge bull buffalo engage in battle. They would spar off and a loud crashing of horns would fill the night air as the two behemoths crashed together. Even the rhino fought with each other on occasion. If one approached another too closely without first sniffing and jostling horns there would be a brief battle. One rhino had a huge rip in his skin from a fight with either another rhino or a buffalo. Sometimes the rhinos would click their horns together as sort of a greeting to one another. The whole scene seemed unreal, almost like a dream. The animals would appear and disappear quietly like ghosts in the night.

The animals would sometimes go away until there were only a few in the lighted area. Then, at the very edge of the light, you could make out huge, monster-like forms with your binoculars. As they slowly walked out into the light, the full shape of their body materialized as they drew closer to you. Sometimes they would pause for a considerable time before walking down to the salt lick. The two girls were so glad we woke them up, as it was the first time they had seen and heard elephant trumpet. Then we saw a huge battle. A big buffalo got too close to a baby elephant and the mother elephant charged the buffalo, not a bluff this time. She rammed her tusk into the buffalo and pushed him right to the ground sending his legs flying from beneath him. We thought she had surely killed him, but buffalo are as tough as nails. He scrambled to his feet, squared off, and charged the elephant,

The stately waterbuck was one of the first animals we saw from the roof.

A rare forest antelope walked into the scene.

A huge wart hog walked directly beneath us. There were a number of them in the area. Plowed up ground in the background was done by rhinos and elephants. The elephants would stick their tusks into the ground and pry loose chunks of earth in their quest for salt. Rhinos would drive their horn into the hard packed earth, then bend their head back until the earth gave way. We watched them for hours on end, mostly after dark when the real show began.

Two huge buffalo parade directly beneath us at Treetops.

lowering his massive horns for the battle. Then the elephant rushed at the buffalo at full speed with a tremendous trumpeting roar that shook the whole camp. Anyone who had tried to sleep was blasted wide awake as it occurred right underneath the rooms. The buffalo turned tail and ran and the elephant chased it far into the woods trumpeting and roaring so that she could be heard for miles around. If I only had brought flashbulbs, I could have captured the scene on film.

The rhino seem to challenge everything, probably because of their poor eyesight. They go strictly by smell and constantly sniff the air. If they detect the odor of another animal too closely, they will snort loudly at it—a warning for the animal not to come any

closer or there will be trouble. But none of the big animals flee in panic when confronted by another. The buffalo stand their ground, automatically lowering their huge heads and presenting their enormous horns in a most effective pose for a show of strength. They rarely retreat nor do they come any closer. They seem to set a minimum distance at which they will tolerate the approach of another animal, even their own kind. If the animal gets any closer, then a fight may ensue. However, the buffalo always back off when the elephants move in, as does everything else.

We saw a few smaller animals move into the circle of light from time to time. There were several bushbuck, waterbuck, antelopes of an undetermined spe-

Snow-covered Mt. Kenya at dusk as seen from the Treetops Hotel. Though we were practically on the equator we had to wear heavy sweaters or coats to keep from freezing.

very first time I had heard of it—so I decided to stay up as long as possible and enjoy it to the fullest. But after the animals also decided it was time to go to bed and drifted off into the forest, there were only a few buffalo and the four original rhino in the arena. Then two more rhinos joined the scene—one with two huge horns that were jet black and very pointed, the front horn over two feet long—so there was a total of six at the lick at one time.

As much as I enjoyed the show, the cold air was getting to me and I was growing tired and sleepy. Finally at 1:00 A.M. I decided I had enough and went off to bed, where I immediately fell asleep. It had been a fascinating adventure, a highlight of the tour.

Saturday, Oct. 4

I slept like a log but still got up at dawn to look for wildlife. However, there wasn't much about except for a few buffalo. The songs of many birds filled the early morning air and one man was up on the roof making a tape recording. We had coffee and rolls for breakfast and left Treetops at 8:30 A.M., again by land rovers. I sort of hated to leave the place, I had enjoyed it so much. We rode back to the Outspan Hotel for our regular breakfast of bacon, eggs, and the usual fruit juice or whatever you liked. Then we moved on to our next stop, the luxurious Mt. Kenya Safari Club, a millionaire resort partly owned by actor William Holden.

cies, and even a rabbit, who ran in among the elephants. He seemed a little out of place with the huge beasts. We also saw a strange badger-like creature and a few other small animals that could not be identified in the dim light. It was now getting late and things quieted down for the night. Most of the elephants had gone. It was approaching midnight as one by one the audience drifted off to bed. Soon I was all alone and I had the whole show to myself. I had wanted to visit Treetops for many years—since the

6. Mt. Kenya Safari Club—Amboseli— Mt. Kilimanjaro

The Mt. Kenya Safari club is practically on the equator. In fact we stopped at the equator line, which is marked by a large sign at Nanyuki. I was wearing a sweater most of the morning, for even here the air is quite cold in the early part of the day because of the fairly high altitude. I saw a few small herds of hartebeest and gazelle on the way to the club, but the

area was nearly all domesticated and fenced and the small amount of game we saw was insignificant. Our guide said that it was protected and that they hoped to build up the game in future years. However I have heard that much of it is killed by poachers even in the parks, let alone the small amount that somehow survives outside. We reached the gates to the club shortly

Flower gardens and spacious lawns surround the Mt. Kenya Safari Club with neat cottages.

The author plays with a tame ground hornbill at the Mt. Kenya Safari Club.

before noon. The area around the Safari Club is a small game preserve and we saw a number of ostrich, eland, zebra, impala, and giraffe almost as soon as we were inside the gates. They were all very tame and scarcely moved out of the way. They made good photo subjects.

We drove up to the main lodge and were assigned to our rooms, which even surpassed the beautiful ones in Zambia or Jo-Burg. They were immaculately clean, with large fluffy rugs on the floor and a fireplace. The beds were extremely comfortable and the rooms were handsomely decorated with animal skins. On the wall a huge plaque of skins made from the beautiful colobus monkey was the center theme. I felt a bit sad at this for I knew that a dozen or so of these rare monkeys had to die to make the decoration. A carved wooden animal or native mask would have been just as suitable. I looked around the room briefly marveling at the luxury, then grabbed a couple of cameras and went out to explore the grounds, which were even more beautiful than the rooms.

First of all, there was a stunning view of snow-capped Mt. Kenya right from the back door. The entire area was landscaped with magnificent lawns and gardens. The swimming pool, set on a slight hill with the mountains for a background, is one of the prettiest I have seen. The area all about the club is wild and undeveloped. It looks like the club was built right at the very edge of the wilderness, a choice selection for such a place. Flowers and colorful shrubs were very prominent. Exotic crowned cranes, peacocks, storks, and all kinds of colorful birds strutted about, scarcely moving out of your way. I got some wonderful pictures of them. There was one huge bird, a ground hornbill,

At the Safari Club, the eland were so tame and came so close you had to back up to get them into the picture.

who followed us all over the place. He was adorably tame, and whenever we stopped to look at something he would settle down by our feet and start throwing dirt up on his back or scratch in the sand. He would even let the ladies stroke his huge eyelashes, which were over half an inch long. We called him Elmer, and he was quite a pet.

There were some pet cheetah at the club but these were in a large fenced area, otherwise they would have made short work of all the exotic birds. They were trying to breed them. There were a large number of animals on the grounds and you could take a small safari ride out among them for a nominal fee. I didn't take it as I felt a little sick at the time but some of the group who did said it was very enjoyable. They said they had all kinds of tame animals, including a warthog who wanted everyone to pet him all the time. One lady said he nipped at her foot until she obliged. There was a black leopard in a cage, which they had caught in the preserve when he came to feed on their animals. They also have an animal orphanage in the area and this is included in the tour. After admiring this unique place, we went down to the dining room for lunch.

The inside of the dining room was decorated just like a safari tent. Carved wooden elephants were used as serving tables, the seats were covered with zebra skin, and animal skins decorated the walls. The tables were glass-topped and beneath the glass were a couple dozen trays, each holding a different type of native seed or beans. It made a clever conversation piece. Each table had a small table lamp with a little rifle holding up the lamp. There were large elephant tusks at the entrance, and the menus themselves were cov-

An exquisite crowned crane at the Safari Club.

Close-up of crowned crane shows rich coloring. Did you ever wonder where shredded wheat comes from? The tuft on his head could be the answer.

Along the way to Amboseli we stopped to photograph some Masai women. This young girl wears the typical beaded necklaces and adornments of her tribe.

The Ngorongoro crater floor contained numerous lions such as this handsome pair. This photo was taken with a 100mm lens as I did not wish to completely obliterate the background. Those wishing head and shoulder shots should use a 200mm or 300mm telephoto lens. It may be easily steadied on the roof of a Land Rover or minibus.

At Masai-Mara Preserve we encountered numerous her of elephant, mostly with young. Our guide was cautio about approaching too closely, for mother elephants very protective of their young and they would attack we got too close.

ered with zebra skin. We had a good lunch—soup, fried fish, roast beef with potatoes, and vegetables. It was not quite as good as the food in the other places we had eaten. Some of the group complained about it but I was content.

I noted elephant-leg stools at the entrance to the game room. I thought these were rather gruesome, as did most everyone else, and could be removed without hurting anyone's feelings. We walked around the grounds some more after lunch. Many very colorful birds were flying about and they would stop to sip nectar from the many flowers. This place would certainly be a bird lover's paradise.

Some of the guests went horseback riding. I inquired about a side trip to Mt. Kenya that was advertised on a large sign by the office. It said that you would go up into the wildlife preserve by land rover and might even see chimpanzee, elephant, leopard, and many forest-dwelling creatures. It sounded very interesting but I couldn't make any connections. They didn't seem to know anything about it at the office even though it was advertised right there. I would recommend that people going to the club look into it in advance if they want to see a different type of area. Since I couldn't make the Mt. Kenya trip I decided to go to my room for a nap. I wasn't feeling very well. I think I may have drunk some bad water or eaten the wrong kind of salad some place along the route.

After my brief nap, I came back to the main lodge where they had a native dance, which we watched from inside the lodge. Then we had a late dinner and I went off to bed for the night. There was no hot water in the room for some reason so I had to take a cold shower. It was quite cold in my room. There was wood in the fireplace but it hadn't been lit. I think I was taking a nap in the room at the time the men came around to light the fires, as most of the group said they had warm, cozy fires in their rooms. The beds were very comfortable, though, with plenty of warm blankets and I slept like a log.

Sunday, Oct. 5

Today is a beautiful sunny day. I had a good breakfast in the main dining room, which is decorated with wooden slabs, animal hides, and all sorts of animal decorations. We left the club at 9:30 A.M. and headed back to Nairobi. It began to cloud over and looked as though it might rain. I hoped that after all the excellent weather we had so far that rain would not ruin my final safari into the game preserves, which I had looked forward to more than any part of the trip. I was still unhappy that I had not taken the one hundred percent animal safari instead of the tour I had chosen, for although the Safari Club was beautiful beyond dreams I still would rather have been out in the bush sleeping in a tent if I could see plenty of animals.

On our trip back to Nairobi we saw many natives walking along the road. The women carried huge loads of sugar cane, bananas, or wood on their backs from a sling attached to their forehead. The men walked along carrying *nothing*. We saw a fair number of thomson gazelle out in some of the large pastures, also quite a few secretary birds, huge hawk-like birds that spend a great deal of time on the ground. They feed largely on snakes and lizards and are protected by law for this reason. We passed more groves of pineapples, tea, coffee, and sisal hemp along the way. The hills were picturesque despite the fact that they were all developed. Pretty native huts and neat little gardens were everywhere. There were considerable stands of papyrus, which is grown commercially for thatched roofs. I noted that many of the road signs were a little different from ours. For example, a sign saying DANGER—BLACK SPOT would mean a blind intersection or a bad curve in the road. There were high, bumpy areas built into the road at railroad intersections or dangerous crossroads with an effective warning sign, BUMPY STRIP. You had to slow down to cross over the hump in the road. I had advocated the same thing in our own country as a safety measure for it really works and costs very little. If we had a hump in the road before every STOP sign, people would *have* to stop at the signs, averting many accidents. We saw a couple of accidents on the way back that had happened on previous days. One was a large bus in which the wheels were completely separated from the body. The other looked like the remains of a minibus. But considering the distance we covered the accidents were few and far between and nothing compared to what we have in Miami every hour!

We arrived back in Nairobi in time for lunch and were assigned rooms at the New Stanley Hotel. This time, my room was much nicer than before. It was very large and spacious with a large bathroom and a separate room for the toilet. I washed out some of my drip-dry shirts as well as all my soiled clothes and then went down to lunch. I was a little hungry so I had filet mignon, tomato juice, salad, potatoes, coffee, rolls and a delicious dessert. Then I went down to the bus for a special side trip to Nairobi National Park. The itinerary called for a tour of the city but I had enough of cities and wanted desperately to see wild animals. I had spoken to Steve, our tour leader, about my desire to see the National Park instead of the city.

Native huts on the hills in the outskirts of Nairobi.

A native home with protective fence of dense thornbush to guard against intruders.

Interesting road signs throughout Africa are perfect for movie fans. They identify the area for your movie and add interest as well.

He talked it over with other members of the group and found three others who also would like to visit the park. He kindly arranged a bus to take us to the famous game park located only four miles from our hotel. It cost us $6 extra since it was not on the itinerary but I was glad to pay it.

It seemed like we had driven just a few minutes when we were at the gates to the park. Nairobi National Park contains an area of 44 square miles and is just four miles from the main Post Office in Nairobi. It contains all of the larger animals of Africa except elephant. Even rhino and buffalo live in here. The park is especially famous because of the fact that it contains enormous herds of animals and yet is right alongside a huge, metropolitan city. It is fenced only on the city side to keep the animals out of the town.

We could still see the tall buildings in town after we had entered the park. We had gone in our small minibus, which was our conveyance all throughout the land portion of our tour, except for an occasional ride in a land rover in especially rough areas. There were narrow, dirt roads in the park and the speed limit was 15 mph.

At first the place looked totally barren, almost like a desert with miles of open ground dotted with small patches of thornbush. I didn't see how there could possibly be any animals here. Then we rounded a curve and immediately we started to see animals by the hundreds. Just standing there on the bare, open land with no place to hide were wart hogs, ostrich, hartebeest, and zebra in huge herds. To our surprise, our driver drove right off the road in amongst the animals. The animals were not afraid at all of cars and we could get very close to them to get fine pic-

The monkeys were so tame they would jump up on the cars and beg for food.

tures. As we drove on we saw enormous herds of zebra, impala, and grant's gazelle all mixed in together. There would be more than a hundred in a single group. At Kruger we had only seen about three or four zebra at one time; here there were hundreds of them, right out in the open. The fact that we were only four miles from town was amazing. At Kruger we had to drive nearly 300 miles to the park and we saw less there in our full day game drive than we saw here in just a couple of hours.

Everywhere we went there were animals. I don't know what they ate but I suspect that the dry grass around us would turn lush green as soon as the rains came, providing plenty of food. Also there was a considerable amount of rich green grass near the river,

which was close by. We stopped at the river and were allowed to get out and walk down to a place called the hippo pool where there were several hippo partly submerged in the water about 30 feet away from us. They didn't show themselves except for their noses and ears, which is usual for hippos during the day. There were many monkeys in the area and they would run right up to you looking for a handout. A huge number of storks all standing beside a small pond looked as though they were watching a ball game as they hardly moved. Then we saw a number of giraffe and were just about to go over to them when we noticed a huge gathering of cars up ahead. We knew it must be lions as this is the only thing that would draw so many cars.

We stopped at a river and were allowed to get out and walk around. There were hippos in a pool but they remained submerged most of the time. The area was very scenic, with beautiful Yellow-Fever trees along the banks.

*There were many monkeys in the area and they would run
right up to you, looking for a handout.*

A trio of zebra at Nairobi National Park.

Nairobi National Park is full of animals, yet it is just four miles from the bustling city. If it isn't included in your trip, it is usually a simple matter to get there by private car or minibus.

Coke's hartebeest (Alcelaphus buselaphus) were common in Nairobi National Park.

Lions on a kill at Nairobi National Park. They were hiding in a thicket. It was a small pride of one male, two lioness and two cubs.

We drove up to the area and sure enough, we saw our first lions! There were five of them, all mulling over a kill. It looked like a family or pride of lions: one large male, two females, and two cubs. The cubs were chewing on an animal that looked like an eland, but their jaws weren't strong enough to cut through the tough hide. We drove right up to them and everyone began frantically taking pictures. The lions were partly hidden by a bush but every few minutes they would stick their heads out so we could see them clearly. Then the big lioness got up and began dragging the dead animal to another location. It made an exciting movie and I captured the whole scene with my movie camera. It was a great show. At last I had seen lions, and I was exhilarated.

We drove around a while longer seeing more and more zebra and impala, a huge herd of wildebeeste, wart hogs, and lesser game. It was approaching 6:00 P.M., closing time for the park, so we headed back to town. Everyone was well pleased with the trip. On the way back to the hotel we passed spectacular highway with beautiful flower gardens both in the center and along the side of the road. Some areas were planted with immense beds of bougainvillea in flaming reds, orange, or lavender. It would make the entire roadside a mass of color.

We were soon back at the hotel. I put my flight bag and cameras up in my room and then decided to walk around the city by myself. I covered about four or five blocks, walking into the Indian section. I was a little apprehensive, being the only white person in the entire area, but no one paid any attention to me. I did some window shopping and stopped at a few tour companies to pick up brochures for my next trip to Africa. Most of the stores were closed as it was after hours so I finally returned to the hotel. I had acquaintances in Nairobi, Michela and Armand Dennis, who had once visited me in my home in Miami. I decided to give them a call, wondering if they would even remember me as it had been several years since I had seen them. Mr. Dennis is a famous TV and animal photographer and Michela has authored many books about Africa. I got their number from the local telephone directory in my room and placed the call. A native answered and I thought I had the wrong number. I asked for Mrs. Dennis and in a moment a woman's voice came over the phone. She was very surprised to hear from me and certainly did remember me and her visit to our home. She is an ardent conservationist and we talked about the plight of the wild animals in Africa. She said she was working on a forest restoration project, which I thought was most interesting. Also she is building a bird preserve of some type. I told her I was leaving early the next morning for the game preserves and that I would call her next Sunday. Then I began repacking my suitcase for the long-

We saw a number of large storks standing beside a small pond.

This beautiful carving came from Kenya. It depicts a native carrying a basket, while one leg is being swallowed by a snake. It was solid ebony so rather than carry it, I had it mailed. It took about five weeks to arrive.

awaited trip to the game preserves.

Then the phone rang and I was told that my call to the United States (I had placed it early that morning) was now ready. I was very enthused at the thought of talking to my family as I had been away from them for about two weeks, but the call was a bitter disappointment. I could hardly understand a word they said and they could not make sense out of what I was trying to say. We would only get about a half of a sentence completed and the voice would become unintelligible. We talked very briefly and I said goodbye for there was no use trying to continue the conversation. I thought I could hang up and perhaps get a better connection, but I was told that I would have to replace the call and that it would take until 1:30 A.M. for it to go through. The first call had been such a complete flop that I decided to try again. I had promised my children that I would call them from Africa and I didn't want to disappoint them. I had tried to call them from Livingstone but the phones in the country were not working in the area of the Falls.

I finally dropped off to sleep and was awakened by the phone at 1:00 A.M. My call was ready to Miami. I listened and could actually hear the phone ringing in my home all the way back in the U.S. It rang and rang. Finally Paul answered. His voice came in loud and clear. I said hello to him and he asked, "Who is this?" They weren't expecting another call from me. When I told him it was his Dad calling from Africa he became very excited. He quickly asked me how I was and then ran out in the yard to call my wife, who was working in her flower garden. This time I had a good connection and could hear everything perfectly. The other call had been extremely frustrating. I talked to Rosemary and to the children and they were all fine, which made me feel good. I told them of some of the things I had seen, especially the lions, and talked for about five minutes. I was happy that I had made the second call, even if it was going to cost a fortune. It was worth it to know that everything was all right at home. Then I went back to bed and, after an hour or two of tossing and turning (I had eaten a very late dinner), I finally fell asleep.

Monday, Oct. 6

Today we leave for the game preserves and our *real* safari. After a good breakfast of ham, eggs, all kinds of fresh fruit, toast, and coffee, I noticed I was getting low on film so I purchased some at a Kodak place right across the street from the hotel. It cost $5 per roll for Super 8 movie film, which included the processing. This was quite a bit higher than in the

States, but it turned out that it was even higher than this in the Game Parks. I bought a strong but cheap suitcase for about $15 so I could carry my souvenirs home without breaking them. Then I walked around town to shop a little before our departure. I picked up more travel brochures telling of many interesting areas to visit. I found an excellent curio shop just two blocks from the hotel where they sold every kind of wood carving and native artifact imaginable. I purchased quite a few items, including a beautiful Masai spear (the lance type), which I felt would be the perfect gift for my son Paul, and an intricately carved figure of a native carrying a basket on his head, which was made of ebony and was about 12 inches high. I had these mailed home as both were too heavy to carry with me. I bought a few smaller items that I could take with me: a back scratcher, a pair of gold-coated elephant-hair earrings for the wife, and a few sundry items. The whole thing came to about $40, which included postage of the heavy items to the U.S.

Then I went back to the hotel to check out. I paid my phone bill—$36 for the two calls. I really shouldn't have been charged for the first as it was a poor connection. I told them about it but they insisted that I pay, so I did. I left my suit, luggage, and extra things that I wouldn't need at the hotel where they were checked for us, awaiting our return in a week, but I took my new suitcase with me hoping to fill it with souvenirs. We left the hotel at noon and headed for Amboseli Game Preserve. We hadn't eaten yet and were told we would have a box lunch somewhere along the way.

It had rained the night before and the air was quite cool. In fact I had to wear a sweater most of the morning. But it was pleasant driving and it kept the dust down to a minimum. We saw quite a bit of game on this road: at one place five giraffe, then a little later a huge herd of impala. All the game in the area is supposedly protected, even though it isn't in a park, but again I suspect much of it is killed as there is no one to really protect it out in the bush. Poaching is a serious problem in Africa. However, the policy of most of the game preserves is to kill off a lot of animals each year so the herds won't eat too much of the vegetation. In Tsavo National Park there is a current proposal to kill over 5,000 elephants by the park supervisors! How can the natives understand that they aren't supposed to kill an elephant when the park rangers kill them in wholesale lots? I think this is wrong. If animals must be killed (and this I find inadequately researched), then they should be killed by hunters who pay license, or trapped by game trappers who can sell them to zoos, or killed by natives who will utilize the meat. I think that instead of killing off 5,000 elephants, the herd could be driven into areas where there aren't any. Surely there are still areas in Africa that are wild and have had most of the game destroyed by man. But to me, slaughtering all these animals is a dastardly crime against conservation. If this is the BEST the ecologists can come up with, I think they should go into some other field before they kill all the remaining animals in Africa. On this very trip, we went for as much as a hundred miles without seeing scarcely a head of game. The area could badly use that 5,000 head of elephant.

We passed through some lovely wild country and saw occasional ostrich, more giraffe, and a number of grant's gazelle and hartebeest. There were about 50 hartebeest in one herd. Many of them were grazing in the same field with cattle and goats. The road was very nice and we were practically the only vehicles on it. Masai country was very scenic, with rolling hills and scattered acacia trees or thorn bush. The land was mostly all uninhabited (for a change). There were some areas where trees were quite dense. This would be a good spot to release elephants instead of killing them. We saw more and more gazelle and the scenery improved as we drove along. It seemed to get wilder and wilder. I was becoming more enthusiastic now as it looked like we were at last getting into real game country.

We stopped along the roadside for our box lunch. Everyone was starved. We had several sandwiches, cold chicken, apples, bananas, oranges, boiled eggs, cheese crackers, fruit cake, and hot coffee. Some of the people complained about it. What did they possibly expect in a box lunch? There was enough food to fill two or three people in each box. We stopped in a very scenic spot that was quiet and peaceful. The reason we had the box lunch was that there were no restaurants or any rest stops in the entire area. In fact, we had to use the bushes for a restroom, but no one really minded under the circumstances. This was one of the highlights of the tour. I noticed that practically all of the trees had berries or fruit of some type. Some had large green fruit (bigger than an apple) that was a type of cucumber. The vine grows into the trees and it looks like the fruit is growing from the tree itself. There were also bright yellow fruits growing on the low bushes. These are called sodom apples. Our

Our group traveled in four minibuses throughout Kenya and Tanzania, covering about 1500 miles in all. Here we stopped for a box lunch about half way between Nairobi and Amboseli. There were no restaurants for a hundred miles.

Nearly every bush or tree bears some sort of berry or fruit. These bright yellow fruits are called sodom apples.

local guide, John, knew the names of practically every tree and bush.

Continuing on to Amboseli, which is about 142 miles from Nairobi, we turned off the tar road on to an extremely narrow dirt road. We were now in the real African Bush. It was wild, undeveloped country on all sides of us and I was becoming more and more enthusiastic about the safari. We drove through mile after mile with no fences, houses, or signs of civilization as far as the eye could see. We would be on this dirt road for 70 more miles. There were numerous giant ant hills along the road and we stopped to photograph an especially tall one—easily over eight feet. We saw some Masai along the road and wanted to photograph them, but our guide said they would be too expensive. He said we should wait until we got farther into the Masai territory, as they would charge less money there. We learned that you have to pay to photograph most of the natives; they won't pose for nothing. I could scarcely blame them. If someone wanted me to pose for pictures I might charge them. Some of the Masai would ask for 20 shillings to take their picture, but we were told that this was out of line and that the going rate was usually about two shillings (28¢). As we drove on through the scenic country seeing many interesting things, we watched a huge black cloud up ahead.

Then the rains came, a torrential downpour that turned the red road into a slippery mass of mud. But it was only a shower and soon we were through it. It actually helped us for it settled the dust on the road and cooled the air, making the driving more pleasant.

We saw tremendous herds of native cattle usually tended by a lone Masai armed with a huge spear. The native herds are a sign of wealth to the Masai and the herds have increased in great numbers in recent years causing havoc with the limited grazing area. Many conservationists are alarmed about it for the cattle are said to be destroying local grasses by grazing too closely, with the result that the soil is blown away by the winds. This of course permanently ruins the land and African game suffers the most, either dying of starvation or moving to another area where they fall prey to hunters and poachers. The native herds are allowed to increase all out of proportion to the needs of the owner or grazing capability of the land, and in addition many sheep and goats make up portions of the herd. When a herd has grazed an area there is usually nothing left, not even root stock of the grasses. This is in stark contrast to wild game, which browses intermittently, thereby doing no permanent damage to the area. Something must be done about it soon for the Masai drive their herds through most of the national parks. In addition, they kill rhino and other animals with their spears right in the parks. It would appear to me that since they do own the land that they could be given a percentage of the park admittance and encouraged to raise eland, impala, and wildebeeste instead of cattle. It has already been proven that commercially, wild-game raising on a given piece of land will produce more meat per acre than the raising of cattle. If tourists are to visit the area they certainly don't want to look at cows. Some animals, the rhino in particular, have been so decimated in recent years by poachers and hunters that some naturalists fear the total extinction of the species within 20 years. Poaching is done right in the parks, and it is difficult to stop it in an area that encompasses several thousand square miles when there are so few rangers patrolling the area.

The narrow road stretched ahead in almost a straight line, clear to the horizon. I thoroughly enjoyed our first long trip through really wild country. Our guide pointed to a large mountain up ahead that towered far up into the clouds—Mt. Kilimanjaro! I was thrilled to see it, as I hadn't expected to at all. We saw hundreds of francolin, a native game bird, but very little game other than this. Our guide said that most of the game didn't come near the road. Also I suspect that a great deal of it had been killed off by the Masai with their relentless cattle drives and their lifelong occupation of the area. There was considerable cover in the area, though, so perhaps at least some game was hidden in the bush.

We came across a small group of Masai women by

The road to Amboseli held some unusual sights, such as this giant ant hill 15 feet high.

single other car on the road. Not much of a traffic problem here. Finally, at 4:00 P.M., we came to a wooden gate with a guard at the entrance. We had reached Amboseli Park!

Once we were inside the park, the road improved. Even though it was a dirt road, it was well graded so we had a smooth ride. The area looked like an ideal place for animals. There were thornbushes and trees everywhere on both sides of the road, a real veldt area.

The Amboseli Game Reserve, located about 150 miles south of Nairobi, borders on Tanzania. It has a total area of 1,259 square miles and is especially famous for its rhino, elephant, cheetah, and leopard. Also the famous Mt. Kilimanjaro gives a spectacular backdrop for animal photos. The game reserve is owned and operated by the Masai people.

No sooner had we entered the preserve than we began to see game: first a huge flock of guinea fowl, then beisa oryx and grant's gazelle in large numbers. Then I saw a most unusual animal, the gerenuk, a strange, long-necked antelope looking almost like a miniature giraffe except that it was the plain brownish color of an antelope. There were several of them feeding on a thornbush in the distance. Mt. Kilimanjaro loomed up in all its majestic splendor and wild game was all around us. A huge herd of wildebeeste thundered by us on the road ahead. Off in the distance we could see a large cloud of dust that looked almost like a storm. It turned out to be a large herd of Masai cattle, perhaps thousands of them. The Masai keep their cattle right in the park with the animals, sharing the range with the wild game.

We drove on a short way and arrived at the rest camp. I was surprised to see that we would all sleep in tents, but they were beautiful. They were set in a neat row overlooking the vast wilderness. In the background, Mt. Kilimanjaro poked its head up through the clouds. What a magnificent place to camp out in a tent! We were assigned to our tents, which were set on cement slabs. They were clean and very roomy, with screen windows and a zippered front and back so you could go out either way. The floors were made of canvas so that when you zipped the door flap closed, nothing could crawl inside. Each tent had a little porch with table and chair so you could sit outside. They also had a separate room in back with a bathroom, shower, and dressing table. It wasn't a tile bath, of course, nor did the shower have hot and cold water. It was a camping shower that consisted of a canvas bag filled with water suspended over the tent. The toilet was a large can filled with chemicals and covered with a lid. There were two bunks in my tent but I occupied it by myself.

the roadside and we stopped to photograph them. First our guide had to establish a price before we could start taking pictures. A price of three shillings per person was set, which was about 50¢ or slightly less. I took quite a few photos, both still and movie. My guide was surprised at how many pictures I took, but I always take plenty so I can have a good selection from which to choose. I have learned to operate my cameras with extreme speed and can take a dozen still pictures in less than a minute if the subject matter requires it. We paid the women for photographing them and then moved on. The road grew worse and worse and was like a large scrub board for the next 50 miles. I was amazed at the little Volkswagen minibuses and their durability. The scenery was still very beautiful, sort of like driving out through Utah or Arizona, except that the acacia trees immediately reminded us that we were in Africa. We didn't meet a

Along the way to Amboseli we stopped to photograph some Masai women. This young girl among them wears the typical beaded adornment of her tribe.

We left our luggage in the tent and went on a game drive that promised to be very exciting. In a matter of minutes we were among a huge herd of wildebeest and zebra. I never saw so many animals. Then just a few minutes later we were staring two huge rhino in the face. They were taking a siesta and as we drove right up to them they hardly moved. They just sat there and looked at us. We drove on and encountered a huge, lone buffalo who charged our bus. However, it was only a fake charge and he stopped and turned around. Our driver said that if he had driven away the huge beast might have run after us but since we didn't budge, we had called his bluff. The area was extremely dusty and every time we stopped to look at something we had to wait for the dust to settle before we could take a picture. Apparently the rains had missed the area entirely. I had to keep my camera tightly covered in a plastic bag to protect it from the dust.

There certainly was no scarcity of game here. We

Masai women on the way to Amboseli.

The Masai are gaily decorated with colorful beaded neck-laces and huge earrings.

The road to Amboseli is 150 miles of total wilderness.

The Tent Safari Camp at Amboseli Preserve makes sleeping on the veldt a pleasure. The tents are spacious, very clean, and completely screened.

Colorful birds at Amboseli, at the campground. The ranger feeds them each day. In the early morning the air is filled with their songs.

A lone bull buffalo in a swamp at Amboseli. An egret rests on his back.

had picked up a local guide who joined us in the minibus. This was the general procedure in all of the parks. He knew exactly where all the animals were. Someone mentioned lions and he promptly told our driver where we could find them. In a few minutes we were looking at no less than 12, all sleeping in a small clump of bushes. We drove up to within 15 feet of them and they scarcely moved, paying no attention to us whatsoever. We all got good photos of them. Our driver would slowly drive around them so that we could get clear shots with good light. They were taking their nap for the day and nothing would disturb them. They all looked fat and well fed, and I am sure they were with so much game around them.

I thought we would use a land rover in the preserve but we used the minibus practically all the time. They would drive these little buses everywhere, right across the veldt, even across shallow streams. I was amazed at how comfortable they were and how much power they had considering the small engine. It is certainly a practical vehicle. The dust was quite bad and I had to watch the cameras closely. It can easily ruin them if it gets into the working mechanism. I would certainly recommend that anyone going on safari carry plastic bags for keeping your camera in when you are out on the veldt.

We saw a gorgeous cheetah sitting on a knoll, keenly watching a herd of grant's gazelle some distance away, apparently preparing to make a kill. We drove within ten feet of him and could see that his eyes never left the herd. It was uncanny that he was not concerned about us. The animals must become so accustomed to autos that they consider them harmless. We all got excellent pictures of the cheetah. Our guide would always ask us if we had enough pictures before moving on, which I thought was very nice and certainly appreciated.

When I asked about elephants we were promptly driven to a clump of trees about a half mile away where we saw about 20 of them, some with huge tusks. They were calmly feeding on the branches of some trees. We drove up to within 30 feet of them and began taking pictures. Like the other animals in the preserve, they paid little attention to us, although they were quite aware of our presence. Some of the larger elephants sparred with each other, clashing their tusks together lightly. They weren't fighting, merely jostling one another in a friendly fashion. We were able to get excellent pictures of them as they were in good light and the background was very scenic with numerous trees and brush. We watched and photographed them for about a half hour, and when everyone had finished taking pictures we slowly headed back to camp. On

The acacia tree, most typical of the veldt, is adorned with numerous nests of the weaver bird.

the way back we saw a caracal cat, a type of wild cat closely resembling our lynx, stalking some small black and white birds. It ran off as we approached but I was able to get a movie of it. The guide said that it was unusual to see the caracal as it usually only comes out after dark. It was getting dark but there was still enough light to photograph it. We saw many more zebra and wildebeest on the way back.

We arrived back in the camp in time for dinner, which we all ate in one large tent. The dinner was good. We had filet of beef, potatoes, salad, and dessert. I sat with two Swiss girls who were touring the game preserves by themselves. Ursula Hotz and Yvonne Siegrist had traveled from Switzerland to Nairobi, where they hired a local guide to tour the preserves. They were traveling in a private car with a native driver and had the whole car to themselves. They spoke several languages and had already been all over the world. They said they had come to Africa because they had been every place else! I was a little surprised that they would have no fears about traveling all through the African wilds alone but they said they felt perfectly safe. In fact, they told me of one of their girl friends who had been all through the same area a week before all by herself. They said nothing had ever happened to them and no one had ever bothered them. I guess we are so accustomed to crimes, robberies, and rapes in our own country that we just naturally assume that the whole rest of the world is like that, but it certainly isn't. All over Africa I found far less crime than I did in my home in Miami, where we really don't feel safe even behind locked doors. In

Elephants at Amboseli. We got our first close up look at elephants here. We drove to within thirty feet of them and they put on a wonderful show for us. Some of them engaged in mock battles making wonderful movies. Note the tiny baby in the center.

Close up of a dead branch of a thorn tree shows the fearsome thorns. Practically every tree and shrub has thorns of some type, yet the animals chew them down.

fact people are robbed even while they are sleeping. Some of our friends had been chloroformed as they slept and robbers had gone all through their house. I was more fearful of my family being attacked back home than I was of anything happening to me here in *uncivilized* Africa, once I learned the true situation. Travel is certainly educational. I would have thought that you would be much safer back in the U.S. and that once you left the borders of the civilized nation your life would be in constant jeopardy. It turned out to be just the reverse.

After dinner the whole group sat out by a huge bonfire that the rangers had lighted. The outside temperature was cool but pleasant. We watched the fire slowly burn down and then everyone went to bed. The cots in the tent were comfortable, with plenty of warm blankets. I was thrilled to be camping beside Mt. Kili-

manjaro. I was too excited to sleep so I got out of bed and sat on the little porch at the front of the tent, listening to the sounds of the African night. It was positively exhilarating! There were no fences around the tents to keep animals away and I strained my eyes in the darkness expecting to see an elephant or buffalo emerge from the bush. There were thousands of animals all around us and the chance of a herd of buffalo or elephant crashing through the tents in the darkness was not an impossibility. I heard all kinds of strange noises emerging from the wilderness. The raucous laugh of the hyena was easy to identify for it is like no other sound in the jungle, but there would be a strange cough, occasional growls, or crashing through the brush that could be attributed to a number of different animals. The night air grew colder and finally I went back into the tent and crawled under the warm blankets. Then I marveled at the total change in our safari. We had gone from luxury hotels to tents, but I loved it, for this is a true safari. Just imagine, sleeping in a comfortable tent right in the very heart of the African bush! Tomorrow we go to the wild Ngorongoro crater. I fell asleep thinking of all the animals we would see in the days ahead.

7. Ngorongoro Crater—Olduvai Gorge

Tuesday, Oct. 7

I awoke at dawn to the tune of numerous tropical birds and in time to see a spectacular African sunrise. As I listened to the many different sounds of the birds and wild creatures, I wanted to stay there forever. It was cold outside but soon the guide brought delicious hot tea to my tent, which quickly took the chill out of the air. A troupe of monkeys followed the guides from tent to tent, trying to steal the sugar from the containers and usually succeeding. They would grab a fist full of sugar and scamper. You could hear them running across the tent tops. If you handed them a chunk of sugar, they would daintily take it and quickly run to the top of the tent to eat it in peace.

After tea we went on an early morning game drive. We saw herds of wildebeest everywhere, as well as zebra and other game. We got good action shots of a huge black rhino running away at top speed. He just kept on running until he was clear out of sight. He was going so fast we decided not to follow him. Rhinos can run at surprising speed, despite their huge size, and they have been known to easily outrun a horse. We came across some elephants, and since Mt. Kilimanjaro was visible we were able to take pictures of them with the famous mountain in the background. The snow-covered peak is often obscured by clouds, so if you want to photograph it you must watch constantly and take your pictures quickly once it becomes visible. We also saw herds of zebra and were able to get them in pictures with the mountain in the back. We saw another caracal cat and bat-eared foxes, strange little foxes with ears so enormous they almost look like wings. They live in holes in the ground and stick their heads up as you approach so they can observe the "humans." We also saw another cheetah,

perhaps the same one that we had seen the night before.

This monkey was one of many that clambered about our tents at dawn stealing sugar from our early morning tea.

We saw two huge rhino taking a snooze right out in the open. We drove all around them and they never moved. They are heavy sleepers.

We saw many giraffe all along the route. There were a number of them around Olduvai. This young fellow bolted across the road in front of us leaving its mother. But he quickly rejoined her as we passed. The sky was brilliantly clear with amazing visibility.

An elephant at Amboseli Preserve with Mt. Kilimanjaro in the background.

A breathtaking scene: the African veldt and Mt. Kilimanjaro.

I was disappointed that the morning drive only lasted one hour. It seemed incredible that we would drive all the way from Nairobi to Amboseli and then spend only an hour in the evening and one in the morning on game drives. Since we had come so far, I would like to have spent a full day here so we could see the place and explore it much further. An hour's drive seemed entirely inadequate to me.

We returned to camp at 8:00 A.M. for a big breakfast and then were off again for another day's driving. At this point, it appears that we spend a great deal of time driving and then stop mainly to eat or sleep, with not enough time spent actually viewing the game. We left the Amboseli Safari Camp at 9:15 A.M. I didn't get a chance to say goodbye to the two Swiss girls as they were gone when we got back from our game drive. As we left Amboseli, I noted that it was a huge prairie, dotted with numerous acacia trees and surrounded by hills and mountains on all sides. We drove right across Lake Amboseli, which was as dry as a bone and as flat as a pancake. There is water in it only during the rainy season. It looked like there was blue water up ahead but it was only a mirage. There were large herds of wildebeest and zebra on the dry lake bed, also huge herds of Masai cattle that would stir up enormous dust clouds as they were driven across by their owners. I noticed that zebras would walk right along with the cattle as though they were part of the herd. As we drove across the dry,

dusty lake bed, it was difficult to believe that this totally dry area would be a huge lake after the rains and that all the surrounding area would be bright green. I would love to have seen it.

As we drove through the preserve, for about 50 miles we saw very little game, except for an occasional giraffe and one small herd of impala. Most of it must have been at the one area we visited because it had water.

As before, there was no traffic on the road and we had it to ourselves for the whole day. We continued on through the hilly country and arrived at the Tanzania border at 11:00 A.M. There was a Masai trading post here, where I bought a fine Masai spear for 18 shillings ($2.50). A similar spear in Nairobi would cost about $11.00 or even more. I noted and was surprised that the Masai still dress as they have for centuries. They wear flowing robes and earrings. The women wear beaded necklaces and huge earrings, six or eight inches long. I bought several beaded necklaces, which were very colorful authentic native handicraft. I found that the spear was made into three parts—the center was wood and the top and bottom were steel—and could be taken apart to fit easily into my suitcase.

We stopped at the border for the usual stamping of passports and filling out of forms. We were there about a half hour and were able to do a little bargaining for gifts while the passport formalities were tended to by

We drove right across Lake Amboseli, which was dry as a desert. In the rainy season the water may be 15 feet deep here. A Masai drives his huge herd of cattle across the lake bed sending up clouds of dust that may be seen for miles away.

We drove through a sea of animals stretching to the horizon. It was fantastic! There were animals as far as the eye could see.

The interesting wildebeeste or gnu was one of the most common animals in the preserve.

At the Tanzania border we came across a Masai trading post, where I purchased a fine Masai spear and several beaded necklaces.

Steve. As soon as we left the trading post and the immigration office, we were back in totally wild country where there was no sign of civilization and not a fence or a sign post for 250 miles. The brush was much thicker on the Tanzania side. We saw a huge troupe of baboons cross the road in front of us and a large number of giraffe. I am sure that there were many animals hidden in the dense brush. A large mountain loomed up ahead. We were told that it was Mt. Mehru. Our next stop would be the Arusha Lodge for lunch.

A young Masai warrior tried to sell us an ostrich egg. He held it up as we drove by. We were still in the preserve and he wasn't supposed to take the eggs there as all the game is protected. But the chances of anyone stopping him would be very remote, particularly off the road far out in the bush. Anyone could

Thomson's Gazelles running across the plain at Serengeti.

At Ngorongoro Crater we visited a Masai village. Our guides secured permission for us to photograph the family which consists of one man with numerous wives. Each wife is given a hut in which she keeps her own children.

A fine cheetah at Amboseli at rest just before the evening hunt.

Colorful beaded necklaces may be purchased from the Masai.

Masai spears and a native mask that the author brought home from Africa.

Masai spears make handsome souvenirs from Africa. I bought the huge lance on the left from a curio shop in Nairobi and had it mailed home. It took about five weeks to arrive. The smaller spear on the right was purchased from the Masai in Tanzania. It comes apart at the center so I was able to carry it in my suitcase.

Hand carved fish of soapstone from Arusha in Tanzania.

At Arusha, we saw some of the most interesting gift shops of all. It was great fun to bargain with the natives. I picked up this exquisite, carved ebony mask there. There were all kinds of marvelous souvenirs at Arusha but after that, we saw practically none until we reached Nairobi.

kill all the game he wanted out there with little worry of ever being caught. This is why poaching is such a serious problem. There just aren't enough wardens to patrol the huge, thousand-square-mile game parks. When one considers that here in the U.S. we cannot even protect the alligator in our own National Park, the problem in protecting wild game in a remote jungle area can easily be understood.

We didn't see any more game. We were told that because the area is very arid it moves out into areas where there is water. We had left the Masai land now and were in the land of the Mehru and Arusha tribes, who dress similar to the Masai, we were informed by our guide.

We reached the Arusha Lodge at 1:00 P.M. and had a wonderful dinner of ox-tail soup, filet mignon, potatoes, homemade bread, dessert, and the usual cheeses. Arusha is a native city with crowded streets and city slums. There were many interesting curio shops right near the lodge and we all did some shopping. They had an excellent variety of souvenirs, one of the best selections we had seen, and the prices were reasonable, after the usual bargaining. This was the last good area for souvenirs that we found on the trip, except for Nairobi. Those visiting the area should pick up souvenirs here while they have the chance. We stayed at Arusha for about an hour and a half, then rode on toward Ngorongoro Crater.

There was a large lake up ahead, the famous Lake Manyara, home of millions of pink flamingos. As we approached the lake, we saw great numbers of giraffe along the way, 15 at one time, and a great many of the interesting baobab trees scattered throughout the area. I asked our driver to stop so that I could photograph them. Some were of gigantic proportions.

We had now descended into the Great Rift Valley and the scenery was changing considerably. Everything was much greener as we reached the bottom of the valley. We saw a good amount of game and I noted that the temperature was much higher in the valley.

Lake Manyara National Park is one of the most beautiful wildlife preserves in Africa. The huge lake is surrounded by dense jungles where the lions live in trees. Sometimes the lake is covered with millions of flamingos.

We were now driving through the Lake Manyara National Park (which I would like to have visited) and were beginning our climb up to the Ngorongoro Crater. We had stopped briefly at a small native village that was uninteresting, consisting of mostly clothes and groceries on sale at native stands. Then we began our climb up the crater rim, stopping part way up to photograph Lake Manyara. Our guides always pick the most scenic spots for photos, and we had a magnificent view of the park. Down below we could see a herd of elephants on the shore of the lake. It was a beautiful sight. There were many huge trees around the lake and the vegetation was very dense. It looked like there would be many animals there. I would have loved to spend half a day there, at least to get a glimpse of the flamingos. Steve told us that the flamingos are not always there and that sometimes people go there and are disappointed. The spectacular birds migrate from one lake to another depending on the food or seasons of the year.

Then we continued our climb, leaving the boundaries of Lake Manyara Park, which is only 123 square miles. What a shame that it isn't extended out to at least a thousand square miles. I noticed that all of the land on the way up to the crater was under the plow by the Mbule tribe. They were even using modern tractors. The land that wasn't used for gardens was used for grazing.

I saw no game after leaving the park boundaries. Apparently it is totally wiped out except in the game preserves. At least it looked that way to me. The road was very bad and progress was very slow. I was disappointed to see so much cultivation and farming right at the very rim of the crater. The way it's going, the whole continent will be under the plow or fenced with barbed wire as has already happened in the U.S. I was told of the chilling plan by two agriculture experts to plow up the entire floor of the Ngorongoro Crater and plant corn there. Some "experts" figured it would be a great agricultural area that would produce millions of bushels of corn. Of course the animals would have to be shot. I wouldn't doubt that this is true, but on the other hand, if the total area already under the plow was planted and harvested and marketed *wisely* there would be more than enough food for all without destroying the last few wilderness areas of Africa. From an economic standpoint, the tourist value of the crater alone is a substantial figure. In fact in many of the countries of East Africa, tourism is the principal source of income, bringing millions of dollars to the economy. These thoughts entered my mind as we drew closer to the crater rim. The gardens and fences continued almost to the gates of the park.

Finally, we left them behind and were in a wild area once more. I sighed with relief. We reached the gates of the park at 5:30 P.M. and had about a half hour delay there; then we proceeded on to the camp lodge.

The area now became very wild, looking almost like a giant rain forest. We were surrounded by huge trees, hanging vines, and dense underbrush. The air grew cold and the road was narrow and a little frightening for it ran along the edge of a sheer drop in many places. But it added excitement to the adventure ahead. It looked like we were in the midst of a primeval forest. We hardly spoke a word. The road grew steeper and steeper and we had a feeling of venturing into the unknown. Our guide told us that we had 12 more miles of the steep, winding road to go before reaching the lodge. He said that sometimes elephants are encountered on the narrow road and that he hoped we wouldn't meet any. Everyone was quite tired as the ride had been very rough for the past 50 miles. The vegetation became even more lush and exotic as we climbed higher and higher into this most interesting part of Africa, preserved in all its natural splendor. Then, up ahead, we saw a car that had gone off the road and rolled part way down the mountain. A large bus had stopped and a group of natives were walking down to the area. We didn't stop as it looked like they had the situation in hand. Besides there was no place to stop without placing ourselves in danger.

We climbed higher and higher and darkness was almost upon us. As we reached the top of the crater rim, the vegetation thinned out a little, but it was still lush and beautiful. We stopped at a wide place in the road where we could look down and see the entire inside of the crater floor, the home of thousands of wild animals. There was a lake in the center, and the crater floor around it abounds with huge concentrations of animals. I thought we would be able to see them but it was a long way off and they would appear as fly specks if one could see them at all. Then we passed the grave of Michael Grzimek, the son of Dr. Grzimek, who had given everything, even his life, to save the animals of Africa. He had been buried in the land that he loved so well.

Now we began to see all kinds of animals: there were eland, water buck, and buffalo all about us. I am sure there were many more hidden by the dense bush. It was now almost dark. We had arrived at the lodge at 6:00 P.M. Everyone was relieved that we had finally made it. The lodge was set right at the very top of the crater rim and commanded a breathtaking view of the entire crater floor. I stared in fascination at the spectacular scene. Far below, I could see tiny dots moving about on the grassy area around the lake—animals,

We drove up the steep crater wall into the forest area. Suddenly we saw large gray objects up ahead. Elephants! They were feeding in the forest.

A magnificent waterbuck poses by the forest on the crater floor.

We saw a huge rhino in amongst a herd of wildebeest. He didn't look very friendly.

thousands of them. I could hardly wait for tomorrow when we would actually drive right down into the crater. Darkness set in and it grew so cold that we all put on our coats and sweaters. Then all hell broke loose. I had gone up to the main lodge to check into my room and arrived just in time to hear the clerk tell Steve that there were no rooms for us. We were all dead tired and couldn't possibly go any place else, not at night on that dangerous road. We would have to sleep four to a room, possibly six. Worse than that, the four single men would have to sleep in an old bunkhouse. The fact that we had reservations didn't mean a thing to the clerk. He had simply filled up the lodge with other people who had arrived there earlier. I guess he felt he couldn't turn them away for there was really no place for them to go.

We decided to at least *look* at the bunkhouse. We walked up a high hill in the cold chill of the night. The air was thin and we were all breathing hard by the time we reached the top. Finally we came to an ancient, mold-covered building. When the doors were pried open Steve walked inside and exploded with anguish.

"Good grief," he yelled. "We can't stay here. This is worse than a prison! Why, in our country they keep prisoners in places better than this."

I couldn't help but laugh. It was so pathetic it was funny. The poor clerk had nothing else to offer us. We looked inside the bunkhouse, which looked somewhat like a morgue. The rooms were tiny cubicles with double bunkbeds filling them to capacity. The walls were of unpainted concrete with cracks in the ceiling and vines growing down *inside*. The shower was so small that it would hardly accommodate a pygmy. Steve told the clerk that we couldn't possibly stay in the concrete boxes. We all left and carried our belongings back down to the main building to see what other arrangements, if any, could be made. We waited outside while Steve argued and hassled with the clerk for a good 20 minutes. Finally Steve came out and said that some of us would sleep in the manager's own house. I don't know where the manager went, but myself and two of the other men were ushered to a big house set on a hill by itself. We were shown through the house by the local houseboy (unfortunately he couldn't speak a word of English so we couldn't ask him any questions). There were two bedrooms; one had a double bed and the other twin beds. Bruce Friedman, John Barbie, and I decided to draw lots to see who would get the double bed. I lost, so I had to sleep on a cot that had been wheeled into the room, which by the way smelled strongly of kerosene or insect spray. I felt bad moving into someone's house.

Who knows where they had to go. I noticed children's clothes hanging in the open closet and we found out that the manager had a little girl.

There was a huge fireplace in the living room and large logs burning, giving it a cheerful, homey atmosphere. There was also a large house dog, sitting on the rug by the fire, who was to share the house with us. He was very friendly, much to our relief. He seemed lonesome and wanted constant petting. We also had a cat that went with the house. One of the men was concerned about keeping the cat in the house with us all night as we felt it might have to go to the bathroom. We couldn't get the house boy to understand us so one of the men took the cat into the bathroom, motioning for the houseboy to follow. The houseboy laughed, thinking that we meant that the cat should use the bathroom. He promptly put the cat outside. Then we left our belongings in our rooms and went down to dinner.

After having hot soup, we then ordered tilapia (a local fish), macaroni and cheese (which was delicious), and roast zebra. We noticed many ants on the table and discovered that they were coming from the very bread we were eating! We ordered fresh bread (without ants) and then the zebra was served. It was quite good, although not as tasty as regular beef. We also had potatoes with the dinner and apple pie with cheese for dessert. I will have to admit that it wasn't the finest meal I have ever eaten, but it wasn't bad, considering the fact that we were hundreds of miles from anywhere. But, as usual, some of the group complained loudly about the food and especially about their lodgings. Then we went back to our home at the top of the hill. As we approached the house, we encountered a native prowling around in the dark. He was armed with a huge spear and he looked mean. We assumed that he was a guard for the home.

I couldn't get the hot water to work in the bathroom so I took a freezing cold bath. By the time I was finished, I was chilled to the bone. But at least I was clean. I went out and sat by the fire to warm up and was joined by the other men. The huge dog sat down beside us. He was lonesome for his master and the little girl who undoubtedly gave him a great deal of attention. We found out that the manager had gone out of town so at least we hadn't run his family out of their home. But I felt uncomfortable living in someone else's home with all their personal possessions, especially when they didn't even know about it. The fire gave out a cheerful warmth, and after discussing various aspects of the trip, we went off to bed.

During the night, the dog would go to the window to bark. We were a little apprehensive as we didn't know whether it was an animal or a prowler that was stirring him, but since there was little we could do about it either, we didn't worry. The bed was comfortable and I was soon fast asleep.

Wednesday, Oct. 8

The next thing I knew it was morning. The houseboy had called us and brought hot coffee to our bedsides. We got up and drank the coffee out by the fireplace, which was still burning. The air was cold but it was warm and cozy next to the fire. We noted as we went down to breakfast that it was extremely foggy outside. Visibility was less than a hundred feet. It was also so cold that a heavy sweater was necessary. We had a good hearty breakfast of orange juice, sliced pineapple, two poached eggs on toast, bacon, and coffee.

After breakfast we walked down to the main building and boarded land rovers for our descent into the crater. It had been decided the night before that instead of taking the *full day* tour, as listed on the itinerary, we would leave earlier in the morning and spend just a half day on the crater floor. The office in Nairobi had recommended this as they said it would be intolerably hot in the crater and that we would roast down there. Of course I objected strenuously to this. I wanted to spend a full day in the crater and have a box lunch on its floor, but I was completely outvoted. No one except myself wanted to spend the full day in the crater. Steve called for a show of hands and I was alone in raising mine. We had been cut short on one game drive in Kruger and now this. It looked as though our game drives would be cut short all along the way. Our driver, John, offered to drive me down into the crater, as he knew how much I wanted to spend the day there, but I couldn't very well go alone. I felt that we should stick with the itinerary. After all, it is what prompted me to take the trip in the first place.

We started our descent by land rover, into the crater at 8:30 A.M., in a dense fog. The road was very steep and rough and the fog closed in about us, adding to the mystery and excitement of the descent into the unknown. Then a wisp of air would bring to sight a small clearing and we would get a glimpse of the crater floor far below. It was like an artist's painting with delicate hues, almost like a pastel. You could see the foreground and a little of the background, but the center of the scene would be obscured with the strange mist. Then we began to see animals in the clear areas. First wildebeest and then zebra would be visible; then the white fog would roll down and everything would be invisible again.

The whole scene changed every few minutes as the fog began to lift. One minute we could see a large area of the crater floor, the next minute we could see nothing. The fog added an element of danger and mystery to the trip which would have been lost had it been a clear, sunny day.

On the way down our local guide explained the crater to us and acquainted us with the few park rules. The Ngorongoro Crater is one of the largest craters, or calderas, in the world. It has a total floor area of 102 square miles and measures approximately ten to twelve miles across. Its walls are 2,000 feet high with no openings in them. The crater is in a conservation area totaling 3,200 square miles in which there are

The dark entrance to a strange Masai house. The structure is made of cow dung, mud, and wood ash.

This Masai hut on the crater floor looks like a huge loaf of bread.

One of the highlights of the trip was our descent down into the Crater. A dense fog hung over the area and we felt like explorers descending into the unknown. Strange trees added to the weird scene.

Animal horns were scattered about the area giving mute evidence of the life and death struggle between carnivore and grazer.

A Masai family with the husband and a number of his wives and children beside their house inside the crater. We had obtained permission to photograph the entire village for a flat fee of 20 shillings per car. It was well worth it.

10,000 Masai and over 100,000 head of cattle.

We continued our descent through the dense fog and mist-enshrouded forest for about a half hour. It was a thrilling spectacle and I enjoyed it more than anything on the entire trip. Our same guide, John, drove us and the local guide directed him to special points of interest. Finally, we saw the crater floor directly ahead. All around were animals! It was as though we had driven into the center of a giant zoo.

But first, we decided to visit a Masai village, as there was one close to the road. Our driver said that we could photograph the village and everyone in it for a flat fee of 20 shillings per car. This amounted to about 70 cents each, which was more than reasonable. We stopped just outside the village and all waited in the land rovers while our driver and guide haggled with the head of the village about the price. It took

about 15 minutes of bargaining and then we were allowed to go into the village for photos. We were warned about the odor and flies before we arrived at the Boma, or village, but it was much worse than I had imagined. The little children were completely covered with them, so much that you could hardly see their skin. The flies didn't seem to stay on the adults for some reason, except for the tops of their heads.

I took quite a few photos, both movies and still. I was surprised that the Masai still lived in such primitive conditions. Their huts, which are made from fresh cow dung, grass, and wood ash, look somewhat like a huge loaf of bread, except that they don't smell like bread at all.

I noticed a dark entrance to one of the huts and our local guide was inside, motioning me to follow him.

Despite the primitive conditions, the children looked quite healthy. The flies seemed to stay on them more than on the adults.

I went in, and it was so pitch dark I couldn't see a thing. Then I heard a voice up ahead urging me on. I was a little hesitant about going farther, but I went anyhow feeling my way along in the darkness. I was in a narrow tunnel in total darkness. When I came to the end the guide lit a small cigarette lighter so I could see. There were two Masai women sitting right beside me. They didn't make a sound. Beside them a small fire of red glowing embers was in a little hollow in the ground. There was a bowl of porridge setting by the fire. I don't know whether it was regular porridge or the standard mixture of fresh cow's blood and milk that the Masai make, but I wasn't too hungry so I didn't taste it.

The women sat there in complete silence while the guide showed me about the small hut with his very dim cigarette lighter. On each side of the women was a flat area which he said was their beds. In back of us there was a straw curtain and the guide struck his lighter again so I could see what was behind it. I stuck my head over the top gingerly, not knowing what to expect at this point. Then as my eyes grew accustomed to the tiny spark of light, I noticed several small calves. The Masai keep them in the hut to protect them from lions and hyenas. Also they furnish heat, for it is very cold at night here. I hoped that the little cigarette lighter wouldn't go out as I groped about the hut trying to find the exit. I don't know what those Masai women would have done if I had grabbed one of them in the darkness while trying to feel my way around. Who knows, maybe I would have had to marry her!

I finally got out of the dark hut and could breathe fresh air once more. I am glad I didn't stay for lunch. It was an incredibly dirty place but it was interesting to say the least. I took a few more photos but there were so many flies they made photography difficult, as they were now crawling all over us. We were told that the Masai suffer from a blinding eye disease and I can easily understand that with that many flies around they could have all kinds of disease problems. But these people live this way by choice. Some of them even go to college and return to live in this primitive fashion. Outside of the flies and the dung houses their way of life does have its compensations. They are a free people with thousands of square miles of beautiful land upon which to roam. They probably pay little or no taxes and the paper work in their life is totally non-existent. When one compares this to the pure rat-race of everyday life in our modern city it looks more inviting all the time. (I wonder how one goes about becoming a Masai, ten wives and all that?) I would not doubt that despite their primitive ways, they

probably have as long a life expectancy as we do.

Everyone in the group was in a hurry to get away from the village as the flies were swarming all over us and we were concerned that we might contract some rare or local disease. I didn't mind that we left hurriedly as I was anxious to see the animals. In less than a minute there were thousands of them in every direction. We saw huge herds of wildebeest, zebra, gazelles, and all types of smaller animals including hyena and jackals. Whichever way you aimed your camera there would be animals. The fog had lifted just high enough to permit clear vision and good light. It hung about half way up the crater wall making an interesting backdrop for photos. Then we saw two huge animals up ahead. At first we couldn't tell what they were, but as we drew closer there was no doubt as to their identity. Black rhinos! We drove right up to them and they immediately turned to face us, pointing their huge horns, ready for an immediate charge should we get too close. We all got excellent photos of them. They were magnificent specimens, and in perfect light too. When everyone had finished photographing them we moved on and encountered a large herd of thompson's gazelle, a beautiful little animal. They ran across our path, twitching their little tails rapidly as they always do.

Next we came across lions sitting right out in the middle of the open plains. There was a huge male with a lioness, who was washing her with his tongue. It was a friendly sight. They looked just like two big house cats. We drove to within 15 feet of them and they ignored us completely. After the big lion finished washing his mate, he simply rolled over and went to sleep. It made a great movie. We drove on a little further and found another large male sitting by himself. He had an exceptionally large mane, with a lot of black around the edges. We drove to within ten feet of him and the cameras clicked almost in unison. This is certainly an animal photographer's paradise. If you can't get good animal pictures here, then you couldn't get them anywhere. There are animals every place you look.

Every place we went there would be large herds of wildebeest running on both sides of the land rover. The crater floor was a huge place. It looked very small from the top but once you get down inside it is immense. I noticed the other land rovers around us from time to time and it made photos more interesting to include them. The scenery around the crater wall is quite spectacular, with beautiful forests along the base in some areas, allowing for a changing background in many of the photos. The inside of the crater itself is so huge that you can hardly see the far side. Photo-

We saw two very large animals up ahead. Black rhinos! It was a mother with a half grown calf. Note the magnificent horn.

graphic possibilities were such that I took roll after roll of both movie and still pictures.

We saw two wildebeest fighting savagely in the distance and approached them with the idea of taking movies of the action. They stopped fighting as we neared them and waited until we were about 40 feet away and were in position for pictures. Then, as if on cue, they started fighting again, crashing heads together and pushing each other to the ground. We were able to get excellent movies of the battle. The crater floor is a good place for studying animal behavior. If you spent enough time there you could just about cover every phase of wild animal life, from birth to death. You could easily cover lion or hyena kills. It would simply be a matter of locating the pride of lions with binoculars, approaching them within camera range, and simply sitting there and waiting for the kill. There were no trees or shrubs in the main part of the crater so that all the action would be clearly visible from start to finish.

We saw a huge lone rhino walking in amongst a large herd of zebra and wildebeest. As we stopped to photograph him, he would point his huge horn directly at us. He was very alert and I thought he would charge any minute. Another land rover approached him from the side and it looked as though he would charge them, for they slowly drew closer to him. It would have made an excellent movie but instead of charging, the

rhino trotted off in the opposite direction and was soon lost among the multitude of animals. As we moved on, edging slowly through enormous herds of game, we came to the lake. There were a few hippo there and we were allowed to get out of the vehicle to observe them on foot. They were quite a distance from shore and partly submerged so we couldn't get satisfactory photos of them. But it was interesting just to walk along the shore of the lake. We were told that the hippos somehow got into the lake by themselves. They must have walked in by the road as this is the only way into the crater. We drove on around the lake and encountered small flocks of the spectacular pink flamingos standing in the water close to shore. We drove in close to them to make them fly so we could take movies of them in flight. This was much more beautiful than taking them simply standing in the water. The beautiful black and pink of their wings would show up as they flew, making a pretty scene for movies.

There were many hyena along the shore of the lake. At one spot we saw 13. They were just basking in the sunlight, next to the water, and would get up and run away with their peculiar hunched gait as we approached. We also saw ostrich, graceful waterbucks, jackals, and bat-eared foxes as we slowly made our way across the crater floor. The ground was very rough, pitted with holes made from the animal hoofs, so we had to proceed very slowly in order to avoid a very

A land rover approached this black rhino from the side and he pointed his huge horn at the vehicle—as if he might charge.

A herd of Wildebeeste in the Ngorongoro Crater. A strange, dense cloud hung over us, adding to the fascination of this amazing place.

A trio of wildebeest at Ngorongoro.

bumpy ride.

I found that my Alpa camera with the wide angle lens and the Minolta with its 100mm lens gave me perfect coverage of all the wildlife. I used the Alpa for over-all shots where I wanted to take in the entire scene to show the large masses of animals or the slopes of the crater wall behind. Then I used the Minolta with its 4″ telephoto lens for general animal shots. It worked· perfectly. The Minolta, with its fast reflex focusing had built-in exposure meter, enabled me to take several good shots of each animal when I felt it was worthwhile. The through-the-lens focusing, where you see exactly what you are getting and whether or not it is in focus, is fabulous. I was able to get sometimes four or five different views of the animal, quickly and easily, before it had time to turn around. Usually they would be ten to 20 feet away from our land

rover when we stopped for pictures. The 4″ lens of the Minolta brought them in just close enough to allow for a little composition around the animal. Sometimes it would bring them in too close, but most of the time it was perfect. If you want real closeup shots, then you should use a 6″ or 8″ lens, steadying it on the roof of the land rover.

I found very little use for my 12″ telephoto lens. You certainly could not use it effectively in a bouncing land rover. You really need a tripod for it. Besides, the guides usually bring you so close to the animals that you wouldn't even be able to focus on them with a 12″ lens. Even if you could, you would only get a small portion of the animal into your viewfinder. I would say that a large telephoto lens is not needed at all for general photography in the game preserves. The only place where it would prove useful would be in and around game lodges, where there were many trees. Here a 12″ or longer lens would be useful for photographing birds. There are many spectacular birds in Africa but you could not photograph them very well from a land rover unless you had the vehicle to yourself so that you could take your time and use a tripod. The other exception to long-range photography would be for action shots of animal kills. Here again you would really need your own land rover; or you could attend a special photo safari where the driver and occupants would be willing to sit and wait—hours or even days—for the choice events to occur.

I used mostly Kodachrome II and high-speed Ektachrome in my still cameras, with preference for the former. I would judge the available light as to the choice of film, and I found that with the telephoto lens the Hi-Speed Ektachrome would allow me to use a higher f: stop as well as shutter speed so that the resulting photo would have greater depth of field. I think that for many subjects, particularly animals, the difference in color between the two films is not that great and the high speed film will often give better results, but this is a matter of preference. However, for a photo where extreme color accuracy is needed, I would select the Kodachrome II.

We drove on and on through the sea of animals, stopping whenever we came across something new or whenever one of us wanted to take a photo of some particular thing. Our guide, John, was most accommodating in this respect, always glad to stop whenever we wanted to take a picture. He would always ask if everyone was finished before moving the vehicle, which otherwise would have ruined the shot, particularly movies. Just imagine how your movies would look if the driver started the car into motion while you were still filming. There would be a wobbling of

There were a number of flamingos in the crater lake and as we approached they often took to the air, making a beautiful scene for movies.

A hyena on the watch at the crater.

the scene after every shot, which would greatly detract from the quality of the finished film.

It was now approaching noon so we headed into a small forested area along the edge of the crater floor. The trees were yellow fever trees, a species indigenous to the area that gets its name from its bright yellow bark. We stopped here for hot tea and coffee and were allowed to walk around to explore the immediate area. Hundreds of pretty birds serenaded us from the trees above, as some larger ones would swoop down to take food from another group who were having a box lunch in this beautiful spot. It was so *hot* that I had to keep my sweater on so I wouldn't freeze. We stayed there for about a half hour and then headed back up the crater rim.

The ride up was as equally spectacular as the ride into the crater, despite the fact that the fog had finally vanished. Now we could see for miles around. I noted that the walls of the crater consisted of dense forests and heavy brush. There were smaller forests right down on the crater floor providing shade and security for the animals when they desired it. The good-sized lake had several small streams or springs emptying into it, providing a constant source of water. Animal lovers should be forever grateful to those who worked to preserve this fantastic area in its completely natural condition.

It remained cold practically all of the day and the hot, torrid weather that was supposed to roast us alive never materialized. Apparently the early morning fog had something to do with the cold weather, for Steve said that the last time he was there it was "beastly" hot.

We continued up the crater wall, a slow, gradual climb as the road more or less followed natural flattened areas. We had gone just a short way when we suddenly saw a large gray object in the forest ahead. Elephants! They were feeding right alongside the road. We stopped for photos and were less than 25 feet away from one huge elephant. He kept on feeding but eyed us cautiously, flapping his ears a few times as if to tell us not to approach any closer. We were so close to the huge beast that I couldn't get the whole animal in the viewfinder of my camera. The scene was especially nice because we were now in the rich green forest, which made an interesting background for the animals. It was one of the prettiest elephant scenes I had observed on the whole safari. There were several of the magnificent beasts, some further away in the woods, and we could watch them feed and pull down brush from the lower branches of the trees. They certainly didn't appear to be damaging the forests very much. The thinning out of vegetation that they do probably helps the area. One of the elephants with only one tusk let us photograph it without moving away from the area. I am sure everyone got good photos as the light was perfect. You couldn't get much closer to an elephant than this!

As we moved on we soon saw a large troupe of baboons up ahead. One of them was a huge male and probably the leader of the group. We photographed them amid the luxurious jungle growth of the area. Then we continued on up the crater wall. Now that we could see the road in good light, it was rather hair-raising. On one side it would drop off to a sheer cliff over a thousand feet down. We could look down at the other land rovers following us and they looked like tiny toys. The road ahead and behind us looked like a black line painted into the wall of the crater. As we looked up we wondered how our land rover could possibly climb the steep, narrow trail. We stopped near the top to take pictures of the crater, then we drove on back to the lodge in time for lunch. It was now 1:00 P.M. We had been in the crater only four and a half hours. I still would like to have spent a full day down there.

The dinner was fair. We had macaroni and cheese with tuna fish mixed in it. It was good but it looked suspiciously like the same food left over from the night before. There was also chicken, fried potatoes, vegetables, and dessert. We were assigned new rooms. This time I drew a double room, sharing it with John Bar-

The rich grass provides fodder for the thousands of large animals in the crater, especially these zebra and wildebeest.

The crater rim at Ngorongoro. There is no natural pass through the wall. The dark line on the wall at the right is the road we took out of the crater.

A majestic waterbuck stands in front of an acacia tree forest at the foot of the crater wall.

An elephant in the forest at Ngorongoro Crater.

Hindsight is better than foresight, at least as far as these zebras are concerned. They ignore us as they graze contentedly on the Ngorongoro Crater floor.

A large black-maned lion at Ngorongoro. Here the king of beasts is surrounded by many animals and food is never a problem. His only worry is the Masai, who may occasionally hunt him with a spear as a test for their manhood.

The Ngorongoro Crater Lodge sits beside a dense forest right at the top edge of the crater rim. The area is filled with huge buffalo walk right up to the lodge at night.

bie. It was a splendid room—clean and spacious—with *hot* water. There was a gas-type hot-water heater that would cut on as soon as you opened a faucet. It gave all the hot water we needed. Apparently we had the same type of heater in the manager's house but I must not have turned it on right. Our room overlooked the crater and we had a splendid view of it from right inside. John wanted to rest a while so I decided to walk around and explore the grounds near the lodge.

I noticed a sign saying FIG TREE with an arrow pointing down into the crater, and I walked down to see what it was all about. There was a small path leading down into the forest. I got about half way down the path when I saw a Masai warrior approaching. He was carrying a huge spear and he didn't look too friendly so I hid in back of a tree as he walked by. I am sure he

saw me as the natives seldom miss anything as they walk in the bush. Their very existence depends upon their alertness at all times. My only weapon was a tiny stainless steel pocket knife. I wouldn't have stood a chance in a battle with the warrior should it come to that. Fortunately he spared me. I guess he was just on his way down to the bottom of the crater. I was by myself and admittedly was a little afraid. Who knows what a warrior would do to a lone white man in this wild area?

I got back on the trail and then went over to the huge fig tree. I noticed that there was a small tree house built high up in its branches, and stairs led invitingly up into it. Seeing several Masai come out of the house, I hid in back of the tree until they were out of sight. Then I climbed up the stairs. It turned

At Ngorongoro the author followed a narrow path down into the crater and found this handsome treehouse in a giant fig tree.

out to be a lookout station for the guests of the lodge. The native in charge of it let me borrow some binoculars so I could look out and see various parts of the crater. I could easily see animals below with the powerful binoculars. I saw six elephants walking down to the lake that looked like tiny toys from such a great distance away. The view was nice from the tree house but I could see practically the same thing right from my room. I stayed there for a while taking in the view and then went back to the lodge. I would say unequivocally, that the Ngorongoro Crater is by far the most fabulous thing we have seen on our entire tour (not counting Victoria Falls).

On my way back from the tree house I met the two Swiss girls again. Their private car had broken down far out in the veldt and they had to wait for a minibus to come along and bring them back. I didn't get a chance to learn the details as they were just leaving when I saw them, on their way to another area. Then I met Steve at the main lodge. He gave me 56 shillings ($8) as a rebate because I did not have a single room to myself for the two nights at the lodge. I had paid extra for single room supplement throughout the tour.

Then I went back to my room. It was now getting late in the day so we went down to dinner. We had hot tea, ox-tail soup, tilapia, and chunks of beef that we cooked in a small kettle of hot oil, Japanese style. We also had mashed potatoes, rolls (without ants), apple pie, and cheese. It was all very good, particularly the cheese and apple pie.

After dinner we stopped by the main lodge to look at their souvenirs. They had some pretty playing cards with animals on them, giving both the common and Swahili names of the animals, and also cards with

African birds on them. Nearly everyone bought them. I found a letter from my family at the lodge. They have a large basket there and all mail is tossed into it so that if and when you arrive you can go through the pile. I also bought a few pamphlets about the crater, a bush hat, and a few other trinkets. One of the group, Helen Posegate, said that there were huge buffalo up on the hill and she wasn't going up there until they went away. We were in a truly wild area and I wouldn't have been surprised if elephants didn't invade the area.

We noticed that the sky was absolutely brilliant with trillions of stars, so I went inside to get my binoculars. It looked like one large milky way. I couldn't identify anything as it is a different sky portion, being in the Southern Hemisphere, half way around the world. It looked like there were numerous galaxies. I would love to have seen it through a large telescope, as astronomy is one of my hobbies. I would certainly recommend that astronomy fans might find it worthwhile to pack a medium-sized telescope with them on their safari, for they could find use for it in many of the safari camps since most of them are located at considerable altitude. It was rapidly growing colder so I decided that I would retire for the evening. They had a gas heater inside the cabin, which we ran until we went to sleep.

So far we have had a fair amount of sickness on the trip. Practically everyone was sick at one time or another with stomach upset, diarrhea, high temperature, or queasiness. I had a couple of bad days myself. We attributed it to the food, water, or a combination of both. It wasn't that the food was bad, it might have been just that we were not accustomed to it. One lady fell on the smooth floor in her room and struck her head on the floor. She suffered a large gash on her forehead and some loose teeth. She was rushed to a local first aid station and the wound was stitched without any anesthetic. She took it like a grand sport and never once complained.

Thursday, Oct. 9

I was awakened in the early morning by a loud tapping on the door—time for early morning tea! The room was freezing cold and the hot tea sure tasted good. After our tea we then walked down to the lodge for breakfast, which always seemed especially good here. Perhaps it was because of the individual pot of hot coffee or the fireplace in the lodge. But it was a fine breakfast and the service was excellent.

We packed our bags and got everything ready for the next adventure. The outside air was very chilly and a heavy sweater was needed. Because the air was so thin at our altitude of 8,000 feet, we all got winded just walking from our rooms down to the main lodge. Bill and Helen Posegate said that the buffalo had eaten the flowers right in front of their room and they had footprints to prove it. One lady told me that she saw two leopards sitting right in the road as they drove up that night. This is a most unusual sighting, we were told, for although there are many leopards in the area, they are rarely seen because of the dense foliage. We also found out, and were glad to hear, that no one had been hurt in the car that had gone off the road.

We left Ngorongoro Crater Lodge at 8:10 A.M. and I was sorry to leave. I had enjoyed the place very much. Some day I hope to come back and stay longer. *Then* I will have my box lunch at the bottom of the crater, you can be certain!

Our next stop will be the famous Olduvai Gorge, which is about 30 miles away. We left the crater by a different road, a much more scenic and wild route than the one we took here. On the open prairies and rolling hills we saw quite a lot of game: eland, hartebeest, gazelle, and small herds of wildebeest (gnu). The hills were covered with whistling thorn (*Acacia drepanolobium*), a small bush with large galls among the branches. The galls have small holes in them and the wind makes a whistling noise as it blows through. Ants also live inside the galls.

Our guide, John Ocheing of the Luo tribe, had driven us from the very start of our safari in Nairobi, even driving the land rover down into the crater. Not only was he an astute driver in whom we all had complete confidence, but he knew the name of practically every tree or bush. He was most informative and made our trip much more enjoyable as he pointed out things of special interest along the way, always stopping if we wanted to take a photo of something. I asked him if the natives used guns and he said they didn't need them. They could easily kill any animal with their spears, even a full-grown buffalo or rhino. They practice throwing from the time they are just a few years old and can throw it with great skill and accuracy. He told us many things about his country.

I noticed as we drove along that the roadside was completely free of litter. I never saw so much as a single scrap of paper or a tin can along the entire route—quite a contrast to our own rubbish-strewn highways. We saw quite a large number of giraffe along the way. I am sure there were many more back in from the road. It was a beautiful, clear, crisp day with visibility unlimited. The landscape here is dotted with beautiful acacia trees, a type that is typical of

Our next stop is Olduvai Gorge. The scenery along the way was very beautiful, totally wild and untouched.

It was here in the famous Olduvai Gorge area that Dr. Leakey made his discoveries of prehistoric man. In 1959 he discovered Zinjanthropus.

the veldt. As we approached the Gorge we encountered enormous herds of thompson's gazelle near the entrance. It looked like there were at least a thousand of them in one area alone.

We reached the Gorge at 9:15 A.M. and were taken on a tour of the site where Dr. Leaky did much of his work, digging and probing into the origin of man. We visited the actual spot where he found his famous skull of early man. I took some photos of it and then I noticed a stunning red-headed lizard on a cliff nearby. I hurried over to photograph it but it ran

inside a hole. I guess I should have stayed and listened to the talk about the old bones, but I found live things more interesting. I figured I could see old bones in the museum. It was interesting though to see the area of the diggings, although to me it looked like nothing more than a sand pit.

We looked about the Gorge for a while and then boarded our little buses for our next visit—the famous Serengeti Plains—another place that I have always wanted to see. I could hardly wait to get there.

Strange whistle-thornbush grew along the hills. The wind blows through the holes in the galls and makes a whistling noise.

8. Serengeti—Masai Mara Reserve—Nairobi

The ride from the Gorge to Serengeti was fascinating. We came across huge open plains that stretched from horizon to horizon. The sky remained bright and clear and we began to see all kinds of game again: gazelle, jackals, ostrich, more giraffe, and rhino in the far distance. This was just the beginning of the plains. We passed a hilly area with thornbrush and many pretty trees where I saw some tiny dik dik. Then it flattened out again with completely flat plains on both sides of the road. We were in the famous Serengeti Plains.

It was one wide, giant, flat area that seemed to engulf you with its enormity. There wasn't much to see there as it was the dry season and the grass was very sparse. I thought it would be loaded with game but later learned that the animals only migrate through the area in May or June and again in November, depending on the rains. However, despite this it was interesting to see. The road was quite bumpy and the dust was especially bad here. I found that sunglasses were especially useful on the trip, not only to shield the eyes from the bright sun but equally important to protect them from the constant dust. I also kept my cameras tightly encased at all times except when actually taking pictures. I kept the movie camera wrapped up inside a plastic bag and put my sweater over all the cameras to keep the fine dust out of them.

We had reached the plains, which were dry and lifeless, at 11:00 A.M. The grass was very thin and the game had all left for greener pastures. But as we drove further into the park, the grass became a little thicker and right away we began to see animals again. We saw huge herds of gazelle on both sides of the road, also topi, ostrich, and other game. We were approaching the gates of the famous Serengeti Park.

Serengeti National Park is one of the largest animal preserves in the world. It covers 5,700 square miles in Tanzania and stretches to the Kenya border in the north and almost to the shores of Lake Victoria. It ranges in altitude from 3,000 to 6,000 feet, giving it a comfortable climate since many of the rest camps are at nearly a mile altitude. Professor Grzimek and his son Michael did much of their work here and put the park on the map. It is one of the most heavily populated animal preserves in the world, with over 350,000 wildebeest, 180,000 zebra, and over half a million gazelle, as well as many other animals. It has a reported 200 rhinos, 2,000 elephant, 1,000 lions, and 7,000 giraffe, according to the park guide, which can be purchased at the rest camp. There are even large crocodile there if you know where to find them.

As soon as we stopped at the park gates we saw animals everywhere. There were a number of trees about the gates and the animals were all sitting or standing in the shade. It made a beautiful picture. Most of the animals were topi and gazelle. The trees were the typical flat-topped acacias that are very desirable for African photos. As soon as we passed through the gates we were in the flat plains again.

I might add here that since we left the Crater, we were the only cars on the road—quite a welcome change from traffic-clogged streets in Miami. The grass was getting much thicker now. Our guide told us that after the rains it grows six feet high and is very dense and green. This is what all the animals eat. The further into the park we went, the taller the grass became and the more animals we would encounter. We saw thousands of topi, gazelle, and zebra.

The plains were mostly treeless, although there would be an occasional tree far off in the distance. There were also occasional clusters of giant boulders or outcrops called kopjes. They look like they were stuck into the ground, which is almost how they got there. Someone said that they were blown into the sky from the Ngorongoro Crater and landed here. That must have been some explosion. The boulders gave an interesting break to the monotony of the flat plains. Numerous animals live among them, including the leopard, hyena, lion, baboon, and tiny hyrax (*Procavia johnstoni*), a strange little rat-like creature that is, interestingly enough, the nearest living relative to the

There were a few trees near the entrance to the park and the animals congregated under them for shade.

The flat, enormous Serengeti Plains. One of the numerous animal trails may be seen at left. At certain times of the year, thousands of animals migrate across the plains.

elephant! I told this to some of the group but no one would believe it. It sounds a little strange but it is true.

We noted that some of the gazelle would stand on top of ant hills so they could see better on the flat plains. They were probably on the lookout for lions or other predators. We would come to little hammock areas of trees and our guide said that these were the favorite spots for leopard. Perhaps we would see some on the next game drive.

It was only a short drive into the park and we arrived at the Seronera Lodge at 12:30, just in time for lunch. We were immediately assigned to our tents (again I had a whole tent to myself), which were set on concrete slabs and were exceptionally clean and neat. Each had its own little porch with a cement floor and outside table and chairs. The tents were completely screened and had private shower (a five-gallon tin of water on a post) as well as private toilet (a large can with chemicals in it). There were regular flush toilets nearby if you wanted to use them. There was even electricity, and a small light in each tent. They must have had a generator some place. This was a very cozy, comfortable, and attractive camp.

As I sat on the little porch of my tent, writing this book and soaking up the pure luxury of wild Africa, I could see huge buffalo a few hundred feet away calmly grazing under a beautiful canopy of acacia trees. They could walk right into the tent if they chose. In fact the guide book stated that occasionally a whole pride of lions may walk right through the lodge compound. Yipes! And me with only my pocket knife for protection. Suddenly, one of the women noticed a rat running out from her tent. Soon the place swarmed with them, and they were living right under the tents. Some of the ladies didn't take kindly to this, until we found that they weren't really rats but some type of a small harmless gopher. I think it may be a type of African dormouse, but at any rate it certainly wouldn't hurt anyone.

We went down to lunch in the dining room, which was so located that you could watch buffalo, water-buck, and other animals right from your table. Unfortunately, some of the group had been warned ahead of time that the food was atrocious at the rest camps so they apparently made up their minds that it wasn't good before they even tried it. They served roast beef,

Huge buffalo grazed right in front of our tents. You could get excellent close-up shots of them with a telephoto lens.

The tents at Serengeti even had thatched roofs for shade. They were on a cement slab and each had its own porch and outdoor table.

several other kinds of sliced meats, potato salad, boiled eggs, beans, assorted vegetables and salads. For dessert we had a choice of about ten kinds of puddings, apple pie, and several cheeses. The meats and vegetables were spread out on long tables in a neat arrangement so you could select what you wanted. A large netting was spread over it to keep away insects and flies. Also, you could have a hot lunch if you didn't want the cold spread. I thought the food was delicious and I ate almost everything without suffering any ill effects. I didn't drink the water, though, and had soft drinks instead. The water might give a person stomach troubles in some areas. One lady in the group, who was most fastidious about her food and water throughout the entire trip, was the *only one* who did not suffer from stomach upset or other illness. But then again,

we may all have had a flu of some type which had nothing to do with the food. I ate all kinds of foods and fresh vegetables everywhere we went, without worry, as it certainly was always very clean and well prepared.

After lunch we walked around the grounds. We could see topi, zebra, and buffalo close by, and I took photos of them to show how close they came to the lodge. There were spectacular agama lizards (*Agama planiceps*) about the lodge. They had a brilliant red head with a blue body and were about a foot long. We could easily approach them for photos, as some were basking on the rock garden right next to the main building.

In back of the lodge there was a huge kopjes, or rock outcrop. Some of the rocks were nearly 50 feet

Rocky outcrops called Kopjes occasionally protruded from the ground at Serengeti.

high, and as we walked around them suddenly a strange little creature, looking like a giant rat, came running toward us. It was a rock hyrax (*Procavia johnstoni*) that must have been looking for a free handout for it came right up to me, even standing on its hind legs when I held up my hand, as if holding a tidbit. Then we saw more of them all about. They would stick their little heads out of crannies in the rock to look at us. Sometimes four or five would be huddled together, each with its eyes turned in our direction. The cute little creatures were even running in and out of the tents. I could just imagine a lady seeing one of *these* "giant rats" coming out of her tent. It would be difficult to convince her that they weren't rats at all but distant relatives of the elephant.

We went back to our tents to relax. This is a great place. You can sit outside your tent and watch buffalo and all kinds of animals grazing just a few hundred feet away. My next door tenant said that a buffalo had walked right between the tents the night before and that giraffe come up to the edge of the tents to feed on grass in the early morning. There were a lot of small lizards climbing up and down the tents, usually on the outside. They may have been young agama lizards but I wasn't certain of their identity.

Next, it was time for our afternoon game drive. We left the lodge at 4:00 P.M. in our little minibuses. There had been a slight rain that greatly reduced the dust, making the drive very pleasant. The first thing of significance was a mother cheetah with two cubs. The

One of the strangest creatures is the little hyrax, a two-foot-long rodent-like animal said to be related to the elephant. It makes a noise all out of proportion to its size. At Serengeti a number of them lived near the camp by some large rocks.

The ubiquitous hyrax was everywhere, even in the trees!

Hyrax.

There were many agama lizards around the camp.

The first animal we saw on our game drive at Serengeti was this stunning cheetah. It calmly walked in front of us making excellent movies, for us and another tourist car close by.

*The first thing we saw on our game drive in Serengeti was
a cheetah with two cubs.*

A bright red and blue agama lizard suns itself near the main lodge.

light was perfect and we got good photos of them. They let us approach very close and as usual paid no attention to us. We were just about to move on when one of the ladies had trouble with her camera. The lens fell apart, exposing the interior of the shutter. I tried to put it back on but it was a job for a camera repair man, requiring special tools. Then our two native guides tried to fix it, and we lost about an hour of our precious time. After finally moving on, we came across a fine leopard high in a tree. We drove directly beneath him and took pictures through openings in the branches. We were shooting through the open roof of the car and I was a little worried that he'd jump

down on top of us. He did look down, snarling and hissing loudly several times at us for disturbing him. Our guide said that the leopards rarely jump out of a tree; instead they back down, the same as a house cat. I was glad of that. We could see the kill of the leopard hung in the fork of a tree.

Then we saw lions all over the place; 15 in one spot. There were full-grown specimens and baby cubs, some less than a month old. They were watching some giraffes that were feeding nearby and who probably didn't know that the lions were right in front of them. We were very close to the lions but they were all facing the other way. Suddenly two huge buffalo ran

Ready for the kill, the lionesses leap to their feet as two buffalo ran by. We almost witnessed a kill but the buffalo ran in back of the minibus aborting the charge of the lions.

Although this fine leopard seems to be resting, his eyes were constantly upon us, ready for instant action.

into the scene, and immediately all the lions were on their feet. As they started after the buffalo we thought for sure we would see an actual kill. The buffalo ran between our minibus and another one and the lions followed but couldn't catch them. We got wonderful movies of the exciting event. I was able to get the other bus with the animals going around it, which added to the interest of the scene.

The whole area was crawling with wildlife. Giraffe were everywhere and we got fine pictures of them from every angle. One huge fellow in particular was standing right in the center of the road and wouldn't get out of the way. Because he was standing up to his

fullest height, he looked at least 20 feet tall. We finally chased him off the road and got good action shots of him running. There were many more lions. One of them had tiny babies (they must have just been born) that looked like little kittens—cute little balls of fluff. It was too late to photograph them and before I knew it we were headed back to camp. Thus, we had less than an hour of actual game viewing so far in this fabulous reserve, most of it done not too far from the rest camp. I came to the conclusion that some of the group I was traveling with did not share my keen interest in animals. My idea of seeing game is to spend at least six hours a day out in the bush so that you can

The one that got away. The lioness looks at the departing buffalo, which was attacked by the pride.

A fine male lion at Serengeti. The dense thornbush provides ideal cover when the lions hunt for game.

We saw lions of every size and age including these tiny babies probably just a month or so old. Note how they blend with the color of the grass.

see not only more animals but the rarer species. Also you can observe them in their feeding and natural habits rather than just watch them as you drive by. My next tour will be one where I am guaranteed at least three hours of game viewing in the morning and three in the afternoon. Our little drive was nice but because we were so restricted in time, we stayed close to the camp. The lady in the tent next to me said that she had seen 5,000 wildebeest in one enormous herd about 20 or 30 miles away from camp, down by a local river. A longer drive would have enabled us to see the same thing or a similar sight.

We went down to a delicious roast dinner and then talked to some of the other people in the lodge. One of the ladies told me that she had been attacked and almost killed by a buffalo. She said that she had stopped beside a small lake in Kenya and was picking flamingo feathers when a huge bull rushed at her and pushed her into a tree, nearly breaking her back and badly goring her. Her husband came to her aid and the buffalo rushed him, tossing him to the ground. Fortunately the buffalo kept on going and did not return or they may have been killed. The woman was hospitalized for a long time, suffering from a broken pelvis and deep wounds. Her husband had severe abrasions from the encounter. I decided that the buffalo is every bit as mean as his reputation.

It was now getting quite late so I turned in for the

I got up at dawn to watch this spectacular African sunrise.

night. I was just about to drop off to sleep when I heard a loud roar right outside my tent. I don't know what it was and didn't go outside to find out. I thought it might be a buffalo, and after hearing that lady's story I decided to stay quiet in my cot, hoping that he would go away. During the night I was awakened several times by loud noises. One time I was almost certain that I heard elephant trumpeting. I got up a few times and walked out to my little porch. I saw a giraffe almost next to the tent feeding quietly on the trees. I thought I could see elephants and I aimed my little flashlight in their direction, but they were just out of range. It was cold so I finally went back and crawled under the warm blankets.

Friday, Oct. 10

I got up before dawn so I could watch the African sunrise and listen to the sounds of the jungle. The spectacular sunrise was heralded by the loud singing of a thousand tropical birds. There was a large herd of about 40 buffalo right next to the camp. All around, animals of every type were calmly grazing—zebra, topi, waterbuck, and gazelle. It was really enjoyable to sit on the chair in front of the tent and observe the wild animals. You could see more wild animals here at a mere glance than you would in one of our own national parks if you stayed there for a month. I remember just a few months ago we had spent over a week in the Smoky Mountains and the only big animal we saw all during our stay was a single deer far off in the woods. Here you see hundreds of big animals every time you turn around. I certainly do not understand why there are so many animals in the national parks in Africa and practically none in our own parks.

A few summers ago we traveled over 8,000 miles by car from Florida to California and through some of the wildest parts of the U.S. We traveled the entire length of Kansas, even going out of our way to visit a park where there were supposed to be buffalo. We saw none! On our entire trip we saw only two deer and about six antelope. We spent a great deal of time around the Grand Canyon area, California parks, and southern Texas, yet in all this area we saw less than ten animals of any kind.

Ironically, we find "experts" from our country telling the Africans how to preserve their game. Why don't these same experts demonstrate a little of their expertise at home. I sometimes wonder if these same experts are the type that are recommending the slaughter of animals in the parks as the means of "preserving" them. After hearing of the proposed killing of 5,000 elephants in Tsavo National Park, I wonder if this is

the sensible approach to game management. I think not. After having visited national parks both in Africa and the U.S., I am inclined to believe that it is time we invite the Africans to show us how to preserve the animals in our own parks. It would seem to me that American parks would be more interesting if they had herds of animals in them like they did in days gone by.

There is really no excuse why we can't have 100,000 bison in some of our parks. The land is there and there should be enough food to sustain them. If not it could be planted, or some of the wheat land could be turned over to the herds while the farmers get paid for *not* planting the wheat. We have beautiful parks in our country, except that we don't have any animals in them. This isn't just my own opinion. Mrs. Dennis of Nairobi said she saw very little wildlife on her trip out West. Furthermore, despite the fact that we have so little wildlife left, our government is still poisoning the few remaining coyotes, mountain lions, and foxes, and there is a move to get rid of the bears also.

Yes indeed, the last stronghold of big animals is here in Africa. I pondered these thoughts as I watched zebra, gazelle, waterbuck, and buffalo parade past me. A camp guide brought a pot of piping hot tea to my tent and presented it to me with a hearty "Jambo Sena," which means good morning. After the tea, another guide brought a large pitcher of hot water for washing. I took a hot sponge bath, made a complete change of clothes, and was now ready for a new day. It is wonderful to be in Africa!

After a nice breakfast, we boarded our buses for the early morning game drive. Some of the group only wanted to go out for an hour or so instead of the full morning. Fortunately they had a bus to themselves. I just can't figure out why anyone would want to go on a safari if he (or she) didn't want to go out and see animals.

We left at 8:10 A.M. and headed right out into the bush. I was amazed at the power of the little minibuses, which drive through the dense grass, cross shallow streams, climb steep banks, and plow through tall brush. It was almost as though we were in a land rover. I never expected to go through the veldt in a comfortable, roomy bus without ever getting stuck. We could take our photos either through the open roof top or through an open window on the side, whichever was more convenient.

The first thing we saw of importance was a huge pride of lions stretched out on both sides of the road. By now, we had seen so many zebra, buffalo, gazelle, and other antelopes that we weren't interested in them any more, as we had all the photos of them we wanted. Now more selective in our photographic needs, we

The dainty Thomson's gazelles were everywhere and always a treat to watch.

were looking for different subjects that we had not already covered. We had quite a few good shots of lions and didn't want to take more pictures of them unless we could get them making a kill or fighting. Lions simply sitting on the ground no longer appealed to us as photo subjects. We now needed action shots for variety.

We continued on through the preserve and saw thousands of gazelle. Two males were fighting so we stopped to photograph them. I had let the lady with the broken camera borrow my Alpa, as she couldn't get her camera fixed at the rest camp. I loaded it with a roll of film and showed her how to shoot it. This way

at least she would get some pictures of the area. I used my Minolta and movie camera, which gave me sufficient coverage. If you come to Africa, bring two cameras. If you just bring one and it breaks down, you are totally out of business. I had even considered bringing three!

We drove by the tree where we had seen the leopard the night before but he was gone. His kill had also been removed. But our guide, John, spotted him in another tree close by. This time he was in a sausage tree, hiding among the dense branches. We drove directly under him again and took a few more photos. Unlike the lions who ignored us completely, the leopard

A handsome cheetah poses for a picture at Serengeti Game Preserve.

The strange sausage trees were fairly common at Serengeti.

was very alert and snarled at us for disturbing his peace. He had moved his kill to the new tree but had eaten most of it. He was a beautiful animal and we could hear him hiss at us. After taking a few more photos we moved on to another area.

We drove over to one of the huge rock outcrops where we came across a den of hyenas. There must have been a great many of them inside for it looked like the rock was hollow. One hyena was at the top of the rocks about 50 feet from the ground. I would like to have explored the fascinating rocky areas, which have a different variety of vegetation as well as wildlife from the surrounding plains, on foot. In addition to the tiny hyrax, other interesting creatures live there. A tiny antelope known as the dik dik (*Rhynchotragus kirkii*), which weighs less than ten pounds, often lives among the rocks. I saw them on several different occasions. There are also mongooses, spitting cobras, and puff adders, according to the guide book. We saw a very large male lion sitting on a large rock all by himself. He didn't seem pleased that we disturbed him. He looked directly at me with a menacing look so I winked at him and took his picture. Then we left him to his thoughts and drove on to look for more unusual game.

We came across a number of huge ostrich (*Struthio camelus*) and were able to get good photos of them. We followed a good number of secretary birds (*Sagittarius serpentarius*) slowly so we could get action shots

I saw many of the long-legged secretary birds (Sagittarius serpentarius) throughout the area. They resemble a large hawk except that they rarely fly, preferring to run along the ground on their long legs.

The elephant rocks at Serengeti form one of the huge outcrops called Kopjes. It is said that the huge boulders were blown into the area from a giant explosion at Ngorongoro Crater eons ago.

of them walking stiff-legged across the plain. They usually didn't fly, unless we got very close to them, but would simply walk away in the opposite direction. I would like to have seen the spring hares, a strange rabbit-like creature that hops about like a kangaroo. This is one of my favorite animals, but we found out that they only come out at night. You could probably see some around the camp grounds if you had a good spotlight. There would probably be other interesting creatures too, as many small, unusual animals are entirely nocturnal. A flash camera would be needed for them, if you wish to photograph them.

We came across a dense thornbrush area where we saw two little dik dik right out in the open. They ran into a bush close to the road and we were able to get quite close to them for photos, which is rather unusual. Then we came across a huge lioness and drove up so close that I could almost reach out and touch her. I couldn't even get all of her into my viewfinder. She wouldn't move no matter what we did. We saw a big

We found a den of hyenas in one of the Kopjes. There must have been a cave there.

The secretary birds were common in the area.

The ultimate in camouflage. Can you spot the leopard in this sausage tree? Look slightly left of the center.

As we passed by a dense thornbush area we saw two little dik dik, tiny deer not much larger than a house cat.

A herd of bull buffalos near a small river at Serengeti. They were powerful looking beasts.

Grant's Gazelle at Serengeti. There are about 50,000 gazelle in the huge preserve.

Serengeti is a photographer's paradise. Shapely acacia trees are everywhere, and with animals around them they make a pretty picture.

lion cleaning his teeth and got some wonderful movies of him opening and closing his jaws, trying to pry some scraps of food from his teeth. Then he washed himself, like a big house cat, and rolled over and went to sleep.

We returned to camp for lunch, after which we will leave Serengeti, much to my regret. It had been an enjoyable drive. I was disappointed that I did not see the thunderous herds of animals for which the park is famous, but I did see a great many. Besides, there is always a next time. We left the camp at 1:30 P.M. and headed for the Masai Mara Game Reserve and the Keekorok Lodge. This is a smaller preserve, with an area of 700 square miles, that adjoins Serengeti at the Kenya border. We will travel a considerable distance through Serengeti so we should see game all the way to the border. My surmise proved correct for we saw gigantic herds of animals on our way out of the park. We came across a huge herd of impala all assembled on one side of the road. Their leader decided that he should cross the road in front of us and his entire herd, consisting of several hundred, all followed him. They flowed across in front of us and assembled again on the other side. We stopped to photograph this, which made a great movie. The impala, which are the champion jumpers of all animals, put on a tremendous show as they rushed across the street at breakneck speed. Some of them would leap high into the air, arching completely over the road with a total leap of 20 to 30 feet. They moved so fast that some of them only

registered as a blur on my movie film, but they did show up when the movie was projected.

We saw a dead buffalo near the road and took pictures of it. Our guide said that he thought it was killed by a lion because it had a badly twisted neck. He said the lions kill buffalo this way. We were just about to move on when I looked in back of a tree and saw two lioness resting there. We backed up and took more photos, this time getting both the lions and their kill in the same shot. I must say our guide really knows his business. He knew practically everything about animals and could recognize them far off when they were just a blur to us. He knew all about the area, having been in the game parks many times, and had also driven throughout Kenya, Uganda, Tanzania, and some of the other areas. He had even been to Lake Rudolph many times. He said he didn't like hunting much and would rather see the animals alive. He was an excellent driver and guide, with a good sense of humor (laughing at my many corny jokes mostly out of politeness, I'm sure).

The drive out of Serengeti, even more scenic than the drive in, was quite different from the flat, treeless plains on the other side. There were all kinds of trees, even palm trees, sausage trees, candelabra trees (*Euphorbia candelabrum*), and various species of acacia. This was a much more interesting area, full of animals. Many would often try to cross the road in front of us rather than wait until we had passed. One time a zebra came so close to our bus that he practically hit it. We heard a loud thump on the fender, which was probably from one of his hooves. Then a light rain fell, adding variety to the scene.

We came across some huge elephants near the road, and as we were taking pictures of them a big bull charged our minibus, coming straight at us with his ears spread forward. We had to back up in a hurry or he would have grabbed us for certain. He was jet black because of the rain and had large tusks. It made a great movie! We let him have the road and when he finally walked off to the side we gingerly passed. Elephants must be given wide berth when they are approached in a car or bus. They are one of the few animals that will attack a car, which they can easily tip over, causing injury or death to the occupants. I read about an elephant that had grabbed a Volkswagen car in one of the parks and kept picking it up and dropping it onto the road with the people still inside. The car was ruined but the people miraculously escaped serious injury. We heard of one man who lived in Kenya who was killed by an elephant. He had invited some people to his home for dinner. It was dark outside and he heard a noise. Thinking it was

We got so close to this lioness I could almost reach out and touch her through an open window.

I couldn't help marvel at the huge, spreading branches of this exotic tree.

A buffalo had just been killed along side of the road. Our guide thought a lion had killed it, and as we were about to move away I noticed one hiding in the back of the tree to the right.

Our guide John Ocheing from Nairobi drove us through Kenya and Tanzania to all the game preserves. He was both an excellent driver and guide. He is standing beside our minibus at Serengeti.

There were numerous Candalabra trees along the way.

Close up of the interesting candelabra tree (Euphorbia candelabrum) in bloom.

his friends, he got a torch and went outside. He was grabbed by an elephant and immediately killed. You just don't stand a chance if an elephant gets hold of you. I jokingly told our guide that if one grabbed me I would holler in its ear. With the big ears they have, it just might make them let you go. Rhinos of course will also attack a car but they usually just hit it with their horn and then run off. They would seldom harm the occupants inside. Hippos also attack cars and there have been instances when they have killed people in open jeeps. They have a mean temper, and are considered one of the most dangerous animals in Africa.

The light rain continued. As we approached the Mara preserve, I noted that the scenery was not nearly as pretty, consisting of mostly broken trees and small thornbush as far as the eye could see. However, every place you looked you would see buffalo, giraffe, elephant, and zebra in tremendous numbers. We saw one herd of wildebeest that easily numbered over a thousand. We left Tanzania and were now in Kenya once more. A very dark cloud obscured the sun and it looked like we were in for a terrible storm. But it never quite reached us. At 4:20 P.M. we arrived at the Keekorok Lodge, our home for the next two days.

The lodge was very beautiful, with pretty grounds and a brand new swimming pool. Everyone was happy about it until we found out that most of us, if not all, would have to sleep in tents. Then the fun started! It

The Keekorok Lodge in the Masai Mara Preserve was one of the wildest areas we visited. Our guides carried loaded rifles at all times.

was sort of like Ngorongoro Crater all over again. There wasn't any room in the lodge so we all had to take tents. I didn't mind because I had expected this here, but when I saw the tents I was not pleased. They were lying flat on the ground in a desolate spot far away from the beautiful lodge. John Corbey and I said that we would sleep in tents so we were moved there with our luggage. Then the rains came—a torrential downpour—and thunder and lightning crashed about. I noted that water was pouring on to the tent floor, the zipper on my tent was broken, and I couldn't even close up the front. Things didn't look very good. These tents, very poor compared to the fine ones at Serengeti, didn't even have a bathroom or shower, and we had to share both with a number of others. Because the tents were in a wild exposed area I didn't feel secure leaving my luggage there for fear someone could walk in out of the woods and take everything. There were buffalo

and waterbuck all around and we had no lights or fences to keep them away at night. I was becoming a little apprehensive about sleeping here. I had moved my gear up to John's tent, since I couldn't close the zipper on the front, and decided to ask for another.

It rained most of the evening. We went down to dinner at 7:30 P.M. The very modern dining lodge was one of the finest I had seen, especially considering it is out in a game preserve. The dinner was only fair. We had soup, bread, chicken, potatoes, and peach melba for dessert. The dessert was very good but the rest of the meal was not quite as tasty as in other camps. At dinner I discovered that everyone in the tour had abandoned their tents and were tripling or even quadrupling together into the few rooms in the lodge that were available. The numerous elephant and buffalo about the area made the tents appear unsafe. This was further heightened by the fact that just a day or

The tents at Masai Mara were in a wild exposed area. I felt a bit apprehensive sleeping there, especially when I learned that a buffalo had just attacked and nearly killed a Masai here.

two before, a Masai was attacked, nearly killed by a buffalo, and brought into this very camp. He was rushed to Nairobi but it wasn't known whether he survived or not. Then we found out that elephants had trampled down a tree right next to the lodge just the night before. Furthermore, there was so much dangerous game in the area, that the local guides carried loaded rifles with them at all times!

The buffalo were all around the camp. In fact one of them snorted at me as I walked by it on my way to the dining lodge. We could even see them as we were eating. I began to get a little concerned about sleeping in the tent, especially since now I would be down there practically by myself. Also it was raining, not hard, but just enough to add misery and mud to tent life. I had moved my gear to the outermost tent in the camp, and the fact that it was the most exposed in the group made me even more apprehensive. I would be the first to get it if a herd of elephant or buffalo invaded the area at night. Everyone tried to talk me out of sleeping there and the men offered me a chance to double up with them. Even two of the women said I could stay in their room rather than have me trampled by a buffalo. I told them that I *wanted* to sleep in the tent. The fact that it was a little dangerous made it all the more exciting. After all, when you are on safari, sleeping in a tent is part of the game. It adds a little spice to life and a feeling of adventure. How could I write about an African safari if I stayed in a lodge instead of a tent? As for buffalo and elephant, the manager said that the camp area is patrolled at regular intervals by armed guards and that they have yet to lose a single tourist (would I be the first one?).

We all sat by a huge fireplace in the main lodge after dinner. I met a pretty German girl there who was on safari with her mother-in-law. Unfortunately I couldn't speak to her or vice versa. My friend Trudy intervened and carried on a lively conversation with them in their native tongue. She is so fortunate to be able to speak so many languages. What a boon to the traveler. Trudy told them about my sleeping in the tent and she agreed that it could be dangerous. In fact it was she who had told of the elephant that killed a man when he went outside with his flashlight. She knew the people who had suffered the tragedy. Practically all of the group came by and told me that I certainly shouldn't sleep down there. I began to joke about it telling them that this would probably be my last night on safari and that if a buffalo did get me, I wanted to be buried in Africa. Perhaps I laid it on a little thick, magnifying the danger, but I really didn't think it was that dangerous or I would have slept in the lodge.

It was now after 9:00 P.M., so I said goodnight to everyone, as though this might be my last night on earth, and grimly headed down to the tent armed only with my tiny flashlight. I was slightly frightened by now for it was pitch dark and the ground was wet and slippery. I walked right by a buffalo, who raised his head at me and sniffed the air. I decided that if he charged, I would duck behind one of the tents. I had practically the whole tented area to myself. The place looked deserted. I wondered if I wasn't being a little foolish, staying down here just to prove how brave I was. I made it to the tent safely and stepped inside, feeling safer behind the wall of canvas. I quickly zippered the front flap closed and began washing up, preparing for bed. I saw a huge spider in the tent that was as flat as a potato chip and rather weird looking. I didn't know whether it was poisonous or not. I also saw a number 9 cockroach, about three inches long. Then a strange frog crawled under my bed. He apparently had been attracted by the puddle of water there caused by the rain. It was an unusual frog and I thought about collecting it for scientific study but I didn't have any preservative so I let it go.

I was just about to go to bed when Steve, the tour leader, came by. He wanted to see if I was all right and asked if I would like to stay up at the lodge. He said that everyone felt that I wouldn't be safe there by myself and that they could find a place for me. I told him I was fine and that I *wanted* to sleep in the tent. That's what I came to Africa for! He said that the tent did look quite cozy and safe. After assuring him I was contented and happy he went back to the lodge. Then I turned out the gas lantern and went to bed.

Huge buffalo roamed all through the tent area. One of them snorted at me when I shone my flashlight at it in the dark. It was exciting to sleep in the tent in this wild area. One time I heard a tremendous scream right outside my tent. I think it was a zebra.

About an hour later as I was just about to fall off to sleep, I heard a tremendous screeching right outside my tent. I think it must have been a zebra because I heard one of the guards come by and yell at it, then I heard hoofs galloping away. I didn't go to sleep right away as I was a little excited about sleeping in a really wild area. I heard loud snorts and heavy breathing of big animals close by. There were all kinds of animals within a stone's throw of the camp. I wouldn't have been surprised if a lion invaded the area. The rain had stopped and things were looking better. I felt very snug in the tent and quite safe. Each new noise I heard made me smile with delight. I wouldn't have missed that night for a thousand dollars! I felt that those who were sleeping in the lodge were missing out on a real treat.

Saturday, Oct. 11

I survived the night without getting trampled by buffalo or elephant and had a wonderful sleep. Again, I got up at dawn to listen to the jungle noises and watch the sunrise from my chair in front of the tent. The usual early morning tea was brought to me. As it grew light, I noticed a large herd of buffalo right by the tents. There were also waterbuck, zebra, and gazelle. I was very happy that I had stayed in the tent instead of doubling or tripling up with the others. Sleeping in a tent is almost as though you become part of the environment. I made up my mind that I would sleep the next night in the tent, even if I was offered a full room to myself at the lodge.

I went back into the tent and noted that the guards had brought me a large pitcher of hot water, so I took a good sponge bath, shaved, and even washed out a few clothes. Feeling refreshed, I went up to breakfast.

We went for a morning game drive. At this point we had seen so many zebra, wildebeest, and other game that most of it did not impress us any more. I think we would like to have seen some different game, like gorillas, chimps, or even large snakes. The scenery in the reserve was not very pretty, being mostly broken trees and scrub thornbush. All the literature about the preserve mentioned beautiful scenery, but I did not see any, at least in the area we visited. We saw hundreds of buffalo, zebra, topi, hartebeest, and impala, but after seeing them right around the camp and at other preserves we weren't especially enthused. Also the area was not very photogenic. I think that if someone came to this preserve first, he would appreciate the others even more with their increased game and photographic possibilities.

We came across a number of lions near a zebra kill.

They hardly moved as we drove up. Then we saw some elephants but because they were in deep brush we couldn't get photos of them. Next, we came across about 12 lions all lying about in various positions. One lioness was even up in a tree, looking very comfortable. One of the lions got up from the group and walked right in between two of the buses. She walked far out into the center of a field, lay down, and went back to sleep. She just wanted to be alone. We drove over to her and she didn't move a muscle, except to open her eyes slightly when our guide raced the motor. The guides would always race the motor of the bus when they wanted an animal to look at us for a better picture.

We drove further and further out into the wild bush. We drove the minibus through very wild brush with no roads whatsoever and never once got stuck. Our guides would drive the buses just like they would land rovers, taking them right over small trees and hedges, even fording streams when necessary. We saw some vultures feeding on a dead wildebeest but we couldn't get very close to them. If we got closer than two hundred feet they would fly away. Then we came across about a dozen huge bull elephants right out in the open. Some of them had gigantic tusks that gleamed in the sunshine. It was an excellent spot for photos and I was able to get my best elephant shots here. Half of the elephants were standing under a lone tree seeking shade, but even these could be easily photographed. One was a tremendous bull with the longest tusks I had seen on any elephant (it looked like the tusks were seven feet long). We were able to get within 50 feet of him as he kept on feeding, although he did regard us with a noticeable eye. I wondered what we would do if one of them charged, for we wouldn't be able to move away very fast in the minibus. We stayed and watched the elephants for a while in these natural conditions. While this preserve is not as picturesque as others, it is a wild, untouched area. I suspect that a lot of the damage to the trees is caused by the elephants for there is said to be a large population of them here.

There is no question that the area supports a very large amount of game, much of it extremely wild and unaccustomed to humans, even in vehicles. There was an armed guard with us in each bus in the event that an elephant or buffalo did charge. He would probably try to frighten it off with a shot, only shooting it as a last resort. Except for Treetops, this was the only park where we were accompanied by guards carrying guns. It was now approaching noon so we headed back to the lodge. We had about a four-hour drive this morning and I was very satisfied (which is unusual for me).

For lunch we had a choice of hot spaghetti and meat

On our game drive at Masai-Mara we came across twelve lions, all asleep. They were lying about like bowling pins gone askew.

"That's close enough" a lion snarls at us as if to warn us away. The author got wonderful movies of this lioness working its jaws, at the Masai Mara Reserve.

sauce or a cold spread that consisted of roast beef, turkey, sliced ham, other kinds of meats, and a choice of several different salads, cheeses, and desserts. The food was basically the same at all the safari camps, and I found that the reason for this is because most of them are run by the same concession.

We weren't the only ones who had trouble with reservations and sleeping accommodations. The German lady and her daughter told my friend Trudy that when they came back from a game drive, they had been moved out of their room, their luggage was in the office, and they were told they would have to sleep in a tent. They showed us confirmed reservations but apparently that doesn't matter out here in the wilds. They were most unhappy about it and the fact that neither of them spoke English didn't help the matter much for they couldn't even complain to the manager. Now at least I wouldn't be all alone in the camp ground. One of the other ladies in our group, Mary Krainatz, also had to sleep in a tent, but she didn't complain at all about it.

It rained much of the afternoon and there was some talk about cancelling our afternoon drive if it didn't stop. I didn't think much of that as this was our last day on safari. It was difficult to believe that my wonderful trip was actually coming to an end. We had been to so many places and seen so much that the early part of the trip seemed far away.

We stayed in the beautiful main lodge during the rain until it stopped and then boarded our bus for the last safari! I felt a little sad about it. The air was cool from the rain and there was no dust, an ideal condition for a drive. The first thing we saw was a large pride of lions that looked fat and healthy. No wonder, with so much game around. I wondered what would happen if a person tried to walk through the area on foot. He would probably be attacked before he had gone a mile. If a lion didn't get him a buffalo or elephant surely would. Not a very good place to get lost! After photographing the lions, we moved into a little-traveled area in search of leopards and other game. We saw large numbers of giraffe and got some excellent movies of them. They were not tame like those in some of the other parks and would move away when we approached. In fact most of the game here was quite alert and cautious. I told the guide I would like to get more elephant shots if possible. I think elephants are the most interesting animals to observe and photograph, as they are always doing something unpredictable. We drove through an area that had rocky outcrops and many types of trees, including the unusual candelabra or euphorbia tree. I got some excellent photos of this tree here. The scenery around the rocks was

very interesting and much more photogenic than the drab, semi-treeless area around the lodge.

We didn't find any leopard and were about to move to another location when our guide spotted elephant far ahead. I don't know how he saw them so far away, for I could just barely make out their gray forms. They were about a half mile away and moving fast. We had to actually chase them in order to catch up. Imagine, chasing a large herd of elephants through dense African bush in a minibus! Our guide, John, told me to be ready for pictures when we caught up with them, for there were many baby elephants in the herd and we might very well be charged by the over-protective cow elephants. The herd appeared to be all cow elephants, which is often the case we were told. There may have been one bull in amongst them but they stayed in such a tight formation to protect the babies we couldn't tell for sure. We did not approach too closely as it would have been foolish in the minibus. Our guides knew just how close they could come to the herd without provoking an attack. There were four tiny babies. We watched them for quite a while and were able to get interesting movies. It was one of the best animal scenes I had seen on the entire trip for the herd walked right past us as if on parade. A few of the larger elephants looked in our direction with a threatening glance as if to warn us to stay our distance. One extra large elephant, which may have been a bull, stopped by a tree to scratch his back. As he rubbed against the tree trunk the whole tree shook. The elephants were on the move and we had to keep moving fairly fast just to keep up with them. We saw another herd off in the distance and still another on the far hillside. We took lots of pictures and finally moved on.

We passed all kinds of game on each side. It was getting late in the day and everything was awake. The action usually starts about an hour before dark, for this is when the lions often make their kill and all the animals are alert. We came across a lone topi and our guide said that it probably had a brand new baby. He said he could tell this because it did not run away as we approached. Also there were jackals hanging about, trying to eat the new born animal. We looked around the area and sure enough, he was right. Lying on the ground right in front of us was a baby topi. Our guide John said that it was less than a half hour old for it was still wet and had not yet risen to its feet. The mother topi stayed close by and snorted at us in an attempt to drive us away. We took a few photos and then moved on so that we would not worry the mother. John said that the jackals wouldn't be able to get it as the mother could easily fend them off, but hyena could

We viewed the game either through the open windows or the roof of our minibus.

We saw more of the strange candelabra trees at the Masai Mara preserve.

A large termite nest 10 to 15 feet across.

quickly steal the baby. They travel in packs, and one would snatch it away while the mother was fighting off another. It sounded like a cruel thing, but it is nature's way of keeping the animal population within bounds. We saw some large storks close by, more elephants, hundreds of buffalo, and hundreds of antelope. It was almost dark so we headed back. It had been a wonderful drive. We passed all kinds of animals on the way back to the camp, the area literally crawled with them. I felt sad about my last safari. I wish it could have gone on for another month.

We arrived at the camp in time for dinner. Steve arranged for a little party for the group, since this would be our last day on safari. He made arrangements with the manager of the lodge so that we could all sit at one large table. He had birthday cakes made especially for the group as there were several members who had birthdays within the last few days. We also had champagne and a very fine dinner. We toasted to Steve, our famous guide who had brought us safely through the wilds of Africa. The party was a pleasant surprise and we all enjoyed it very much. After the dinner, Steve handed us our equator certificate, which we received for passing across the equator. It was a nicely decorated certificate, suitable for framing, and was presented to us by the United Touring Company of Nairobi. Each was signed and had the name of the tour member on it—a fine memento of the trip. I intend

A lone stork outlined against the evening sky greets us at the end of the day.

Giraffe at Masai-Mara preserve. We saw many giraffe there but they were quite wild and difficult to approach. This is a new preserve, full of game and much of it still totally wild.

We saw this herd of elephants about a half mile away and gave chase to them in our minibus. We finally caught up with them for photos. There were many babies among them.

to frame mine and hang it on the wall along with my Masai spears and other souvenirs of my safari. Many little extras like this throughout the trip made the whole journey more enjoyable.

After talking of our adventure and reminiscing about the trip, we went off to sleep. I found that my next door neighbor was the pretty German girl. I was getting ready to drop off to sleep, listening to the strange and interesting jungle noises that added so much excitement to sleeping in a tent, when I heard the loud blasting of a portable radio, drowning out all noise from the surrounding forest. How inconsiderate that someone would play a radio so loud in a quiet tenting area. The longer it played, the more infuriated I became. An hour passed, then two, still it played on. I had hoped that the owner of the confounded thing would go to sleep reasonably early, but no such luck. Finally I could stand it no longer. Hurriedly I put on my trousers, grabbed my flashlight, and went out into the night to see if I could find a camp guard. At first I saw nothing, the whole area was ghostly vacant. Then off in the distance I saw the beam of a flashlight. I walked over to the source of the light and found that it was a camp guard escorting an attractive young English lady back to her tent. I approached and told them of the problem. The lady said that the guard did not understand a single word of English but that she would try to talk to him. She agreed that it was totally wrong of someone to be playing a radio out in a safari area, loud enough so that it would bother others. She talked to the guard in his native tongue and the only word that I caught was "hyena." Apparently she was telling him that I wanted to listen to the noises of the animals and the radio was drowning them out. They talked back and forth for about five minutes. Finally both the lady and the guard walked down to the tent where the radio was blasting, paused outside, then rapped on the tent pole. There was no response. He set his rifle down, unzipped the front of the tent, and pointed his big flashlight inside. Someone was sleeping on the cot but I couldn't tell whether it was a man or woman. The radio was on the table, blasting loudly. Its owner had no doubt fallen asleep while listening to it. The guard appraised the situation for a moment, then walked inside the tent and turned off the offending radio. At last the camp was quiet. I thanked him and the charming lady for helping me and then went back to my tent.

The night was peaceful after that. They certainly should outlaw transistor radios in these out of the way places, or at least require that those using them wear an ear plug so that the noise won't disturb others. Who wants to listen to a blasted radio while out on safari in the African bush? Certainly not me! I was glad that I did something about the obnoxious radio instead of letting it spoil my last night on safari. Now I could listen to the noises of the jungle night, music to my ears. Far off a zebra would bray or a buffalo would snort. A lion's roar would pierce the stillness and many insects and frogs would join in the chorus. I heard a giggle from the tent next door. The German girl was no doubt enjoying the strange noises of the wild as much as I. She was very pretty and I had made a little movie of her by my tent, to tease my wife. I wondered how they liked staying in the tent, but I had no way of asking them because of the language barrier. I heard more noises from the surrounding jungle. The weird laugh of the hyena was the strangest of all, a loud, raucous yell. No other sound is quite like that of the hyena. There were also distant sounds of crashing through the bush, probably elephant or buffalo, and loud calling sounds that must have come from antelopes and other hoofed species. It was a beautiful night and soon I was sound asleep.

Sunday, Oct. 12

I awoke at dawn again to the tune of a thousand birds and the air was alive with activity. I heard a gentle knocking on my tent. It was the guard bringing my tea, as he greeted me with a hearty "Jambo Sena," which I returned just as heartily. I dressed quickly so I wouldn't miss a minute of early dawn. I brought my pot of tea outside the tent, where I watched another glorious sunrise. I looked out across the veldt and could see numerous buffalo, topi, zebra, waterbuck, even giraffe right from my tent door. I heard a strange *rat-a-tat-tat* coming from tiny black birds in the sky. As I watched I noticed that they made the noise by snapping their wings together while in flight.

I slowly drank my tea, taking in not only its warmth, but the total feeling of the African bush, which can only be sensed by being there—not in a concrete and steel hotel room—but in a tent, close to nature. I have heard that the lodge officials will soon raze the entire tent area and I feel this is unfortunate. Instead, they should move the tent campground far out into the bush, a mile or two away from the lodge, so that those who come on safari and want to live in the wild, will have a place to stay. The tents should be placed on a cement slab and have private shower and toilet, as they do in the other parks such as Amboseli and Serengeti, but to do away with them altogether would be a little sad. Perhaps guests could stay one night in the tent and one at the lodge. This way they could take a good shower and rest at the beautiful lodge and then tent out, clean and refreshed. I shall write to the Keekorok people about this.

I joined the group for a very hearty breakfast. There were a lot of beautiful little vervet monkeys around the lodge that were very friendly, eagerly accepting food from your hand. While eating breakfast, I noticed one of them looking in the window at all the food spread out on the table. I held up a piece of toast so he could see it, but I didn't realize there was an open window. Quick as a flash the monkey was inside the dining room grabbing for the toast. He was just as quickly ushered out by a waiter, triumphantly holding the toast high above his head as he was chased outside. Then I painfully remembered that these were my last moments in the game preserves. I was sorry to see the end of my safari.

We left Keekorok Lodge at 7:30 A.M. It is a long ride back to Nairobi and the road was reported to be quite bad. We saw a great deal of game on the way out. At one spot there were 22 giraffes, one of the largest groups of these spectacular creatures that we had seen anywhere. Areas of dense brush teemed with game of all kinds.

It was another beautiful day and I was pleased that the weather was so nice for my last day in Africa. I enjoyed the ride back but did not look forward to the hustle and bustle of "civilization" with its traffic jams and smoky streets. I was of course anxious to see my family but I was in no hurry to return to crowded Miami. I had not missed any of the civilized world. To many people, progress is destroying beautiful woods or a wild area, paving it with asphalt, then building hundreds or thousands of concrete, box-like houses in neat little rows. To me, progress would be to bulldoze down an entire city with its rat infested buildings and plant a million trees in the area, reverting the entire area back to nature. Let three-fourths of the area stay wild and free. Build ultra-tall apartment buildings to house the masses, or large circular apartment buildings that arch through the woods and have a half mile wooded area within the circle. This would be progress. Man will find he is happier living close to nature, even though he doesn't realize it. A million trees would absorb dust, noise, and poisonous city fumes and at the same time give off life-sustaining oxygen.

I was happy that someone had the foresight to preserve all these wonderful wilderness areas in Africa. In most places there was not a sign, a house, even a fence post as far as the eye could see. I hope these areas can stay wild forever and that they will be vastly increased in size, rather than usurped for crop or cattle raising by temporary custodians of the public lands. Man has already destroyed too much. We must stop and reforest the areas we have ravaged, reclaim the rivers we have polluted, replenish the wildlife in the areas where it has been decimated. We can do all this and still have more than enough to eat. It is *necessary* for our own survival. These thoughts entered my mind as I passed through mile after mile of undeveloped land.

We continued on toward Nairobi. Progress was slow for the road was very rough. One of our buses had a flat tire, the first of the entire trip. We stopped to help them with it and it was changed in less than five minutes. The area was dotted with many euphorbia trees, adding an interesting touch to the landscape. There were many Masai along the way, some carrying their long lance-like spears, others small bows and arrows. I wanted to stop and take a movie of one throwing his spear but our guide said that he didn't think they would do it even if you paid them. Then we heard that the park rangers were out looking for the buffalo that had attacked the Masai back at the reserve. They had their own special way of dealing with wayward buffalo. They would drive up to each herd of buffalo, stop their vehicle, and one guard would get out on foot and walk toward the herd. The other would stand guard with his rifle. If a buffalo charged out of the herd and attacked the man on foot, they would shoot it, assuming that it probably was the killer buffalo which had attacked the native, or one equally as bad. It sounded like a pretty good plan to me.

The weather continued to be absolutely perfect, with bright sunny skies. But the road became very dusty as the rains had missed this area. We were taking a different road from the one in which we had entered the preserve so that we saw entirely different scenery. There were large, open spaces with rolling hills and not a sign of human habitation. However, when we left the Mara Masai Game Reserve, I noted that there was no wildlife at all, even though the area was still totally wild. Had it been killed by the natives? It appears that way. I watched both sides of the road for 50 miles seeing practically nothing except for a few scattered gazelle and hartebeest.

The road grew intolerably worse for the next 150 miles. There were deep ruts, sand traps, and clouds of dust that obscured all vision. It was by far the worst road we had encountered on the trip. The area was bone dry and lifeless. Whatever game had lived here no doubt was either killed or had moved to an area where there was water. We saw only one giraffe and a few hartebeest and gazelles. We were told that all of the area belongs to the Masai and is closed to travel except by special permit. The trip from Keekorok Lodge to Nairobi is about 170 miles. We were supposed to be back at the hotel around noon but it took much longer.

We gave one of the natives a lift into town from the lodge. We had been asking all kinds of questions about the Masai, since we were traveling in their land all day, and finally someone asked him to which tribe he belonged. He said he was Masai. Then he told us that his family lived near Lake Rudolph. We asked him how many brothers and sisters he had, to which he replied about 40! His father has five wives and he keeps each one in a separate house with her children. He said there is little fighting among the wives, as they accepted each other. He said the going price for a wife today is seven cows and they will throw in a goat for an especially pretty woman. I thought that was most reasonable, far cheaper than a wife back home. One of the more progressive Masai, he was going to Nairobi to attend school, where he would study hotel management. He said his father didn't live in the typical Masai Boma, or mud hut, and that his family had regular houses. I asked him about the spears that the Masai use. He said the long lance is seldom thrown and is usually held firm when an animal charges so that he is impaled on the spear by his own weight. The smaller spear can be thrown with great accuracy a considerable distance. It can be thrown clear through a buffalo or rhino even pinning him to the ground. After the Masai throws his spear, he then uses his sword and shield to protect himself at close range. He said the Masai have their own language, which is different from Swalihi. I asked him exactly how the native huts are made and he told me they were made from grass that was held together with cow dung and wood ash or dirt. It makes a snug, warm home, but on a hot summer day I suspect it would not be as desirable as a cottage by the lake.

We stopped at a small Masai town called Narak where I bargained with the natives for beaded bracelets and other beadwork, which is the only type of handicraft they make or sell, except for their spears. I bought a huge, foot-long earring and took it right off the ear of the Masai woman who was selling it. I tried to exchange my razor-sharp stainless steel pocket knife for a large beaded belt. I took out the knife, and when I shaved some hair off my arm the men let out a loud whoop. Then some of them brought out dollar bills and tried to buy it from me. I had a lot of fun bargaining with them. Everything they sold was 20 shillings to start and would come down to ten by the time we left. I bought about $5 worth of items from them. Our guide said it really wasn't worth what they asked as you could buy the same things back in Nairobi for a cheaper price, but I felt that even if it

wasn't, it was helping the natives and there is nothing wrong with that.

As we moved on toward Nairobi the road grew much worse. It had been smoother riding out on the veldt than on this road. We were exhausted from the constant bumping up and down and didn't think we could go much further when our guide saw a small sign. He made the cheerful announcement that we only had 28 more miles to go before reaching the paved road, and that the last eight miles would be the worst of all. It was difficult to imagine a road being any worse than this. We had now descended into the Great Rift Valley, where it was very hot because of the low altitude. The bus ahead of us had another flat tire. It had picked up a nail in the road, but they had changed it by the time we caught up to them.

The time went by very slowly and no one spoke very much. Our driver, John, would apologize for every bump, grunting and groaning for us as he slowly pulled down into a deep rut and back out of it again. There was absolutely nothing in the way of rest areas for the entire 170-mile trip so we finally stopped at a thornbush thicket about 20 feet high. What little vegetation there was was covered with huge thorns, two or three inches long. I walked out into the area for a few minutes, noting that the soil appeared to be very rich except for the dryness. I expect that if it ever did rain there, the grass would grow high and lush.

We moved on into the terrible dust and heat. Sometimes the dust would spiral up into the sky for 50 feet or more as we would pass an occasional car. We would all close our windows tightly until the dust had settled down, then quickly opening them to get relief from the stifling heat. It was not very comfortable. The last eight miles were like a morass of dust that grabbed at the wheels as if trying to devour us. There were deep ruts and a washboard-type road that jangled everyone's nerves. Finally, after what seemed an eternity, we came to the smooth, asphalt road. We had made it!

Almost immediately we began to climb to the cooler air of the high altitude. As the scenery began to change everything was rich and green. We could look back and see the Great Rift Valley far below. The air was pleasantly cool and refreshing as we climbed higher and higher to the highlands of Nairobi. Natives were selling fluffy sheep skins along the highway. It was only a short ride to Nairobi from here and soon we were back at the New Stanley Hotel.

We were assigned day rooms in which we could wash and rest up. My room had twin beds, a modern bath, ceiling-to-floor curtains, and a private balcony looking directly down on Kenyatta Avenue. From the second floor I could stand out on the balcony and

The author bought several of these beautiful carved wooden masks in Nairobi. They were very inexpensive and make wonderful wall decoration.

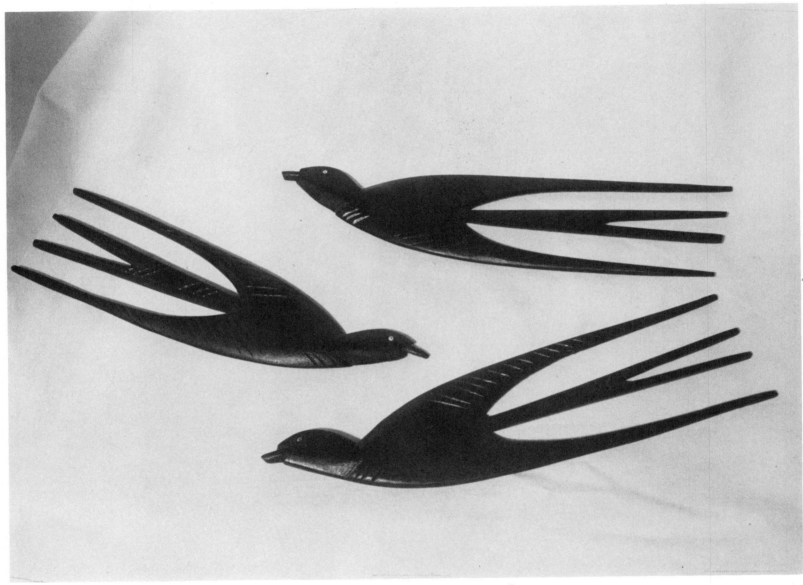

Handsome carved birds from Nairobi.

*This handsome carving of a native woman was obtained at
a curio shop in Nairobi just a few blocks from our hotel.*

Carved masks from Kenya.

Beautiful native drums of tanned animal hides are available throughout Africa. I saw fine drums for sale in Zambia at a native market by the falls. There are also many right in Nairobi and range in size from 10 inches to two feet. The larger size should be mailed home.

watch a panorama of East Africa parade below. I noted that the biggest percentage of people walking about town were Indians rather than Africans. Europeans or Americans were few and far between. All my luggage was in the room waiting for me and I found that not a single item was missing. Even the flimsy bag of souvenirs was still intact.

It was long past lunch time but they held the dining room open for us as we had been so late getting in. After spending a week in the bush and eating at the game preserves, the hotel and dining room seemed like the Taj Mahal, the food like succulent gems from a king's kitchen. When we first came to the New Stanley, we had previously stayed in the newest, finest hotel in Africa and this hotel just didn't look up to par. But now, after spending a week sleeping in tents and washing up in buckets, it seemed like the height of luxury. The dinner tasted especially good when compared to the tent food. I had filet mignon, rolls, potatoes, vegetables, coffee, and several delicious desserts.

We were all pretty much exhausted after the long, harrowing ride from the Keekorok Lodge. It was difficult to sleep because it was still mid afternoon so we walked down the road a few blocks to a curio shop that was opened on Sunday. The owner said that although most of the stores must close on Sunday, a few are allowed to stay open for the benefit of tourists who happen to be in town on that day. He said the stores take turns staying open on the Sabbath. They had a fine collection of wood carvings and every type of souvenir. Many of the women purchased beautiful silk scarves with animal paintings on them that cost $8 each. I bought a few more wood carvings and a few odds and ends. Then I went back to my room for a much needed rest. After a shower and shave and a changing of clothes I tried to sleep, but couldn't knowing that I would have to be up again in just a few hours. I packed my bags for the final trip home, again feeling very sad.

An interesting animal hide drum I found in one of the curio shops in Nairobi.

For my last dinner in Africa I sat with John, Trudy, and Rose, the three with whom I had most of my meals. We had a slow leisurely dinner of fried shrimp, potatoes, rolls, vegetables, and dessert. I was so full I had to pass up the cheeses when they were brought around.

Then I went back to my room to check out my luggage and prepare to leave the hotel. I called Mrs. Dennis and told her of my trip to the game preserves. She said she was building a bird sanctuary and I wished her success with it. It was now time to leave for the airport. I placed my luggage outside the door and went down to board the bus. The New Stanley Hotel seemed like an old friend and I felt bad leaving, but all journeys must end sometime. We were driven to the airport at 10:30 P.M. in the minibus by our same driver, John Ochieng. I said goodbye and told him that I would come back. Once more we were in Nairobi Airport—this time on our way home.

9. Homeward Bound—Rome—New York

Monday, Oct. 13

Our fabulous safari was nearly over as we waited

for a 1:00 A.M. departure to Rome. We went through customs and immigration, with the usual stamping of the passport and filling out of a simple form. No one ever looked at our luggage. While waiting for the plane I saw the two Swiss girls and said goodbye to them once more. It seems that when you meet someone out in the game preserves you are almost certain to run into them again at one or more places along the line.

It was now boarding time and we were crowded into the plane. The seats were extremely close together, and with all the hand luggage protruding out from under our seats it was very uncomfortable. I noticed that since we were flying Air Italia, the plane was largely occupied by Italians, which of course is understandable. It was a very smooth take off and soon we were high above the clouds. Sleep was impossible under such crowded conditions.

I sat next to a man who had lived in Kenya for 20 years and was now leaving the country. He was a telephone expert from Holland. He said he was going to fly to Madrid, England, Canada, and Brazil to look over each area to see which one he liked the best, as he had a job offer in each country. But first he and his wife were going to take a two-month cruise up the Nile to Lake Victoria before deciding where they would live. He was a very nice fellow and I would like to have talked more with him as he knew all about Africa. But I was so exhausted from lack of sleep. I was just about to doze off when the cabin lights were turned on. Breakfast was being served. I checked my watch and it was 2:30 in the morning. I couldn't eat much in the middle of the night and I thought it was rather ridiculous to wake people up on a night trip like this. We could have survived without the middle-of-the-night snack. The man beside me, who was apparently a world traveler in his telephone engineering profession, told me that the trip from Nairobi to New York was extremely exhausting because of the time difference and that it would take about a week to get over it. Your system gets all mixed up. I could believe him.

We arrived at Rome at 6:00 A.M. where there was a five-hour wait before departure to New York. I bought a few souvenirs of Rome at the airport and then went upstairs for breakfast. Steve had obtained breakfast vouchers for us so we could eat without having to pay. The meal was not very good—typical of some airports—and I would like to have gone downtown but we were all too exhausted to make the trip. Besides, I don't know whether we would have been allowed to with our present visas and passports. I didn't get a chance to say goodbye to Steve for when I returned from my shopping spree he had already left. He told me goodbye through some of the others. I said goodbye to some of the group who were leaving on different

planes, then at 11:30 A.M. we left Rome for the good old U.S.A.

We flew at 35,000 feet, and flying time is to be eight and a half hours. As we winged toward home, I could see the Atlantic Ocean far below. Yesterday was Columbus Day. It took him 90 days to cross the Atlantic. We would do it in about a third of a day. Our return trip will take us over Paris, London, Ireland, and Iceland, and our landfall in America will be Labrador. What a pity that the airlines couldn't make arrangements to fly down at about a thousand feet over each of these places so that we could get a glimpse of them from the air.

As we flew high above the Atlantic on the last leg of our safari, I took stock of my adventure. In just three weeks time I covered 23,000 miles and spanned the entire continent. I had a chance to explore briefly the West coast of Africa at Senegal; to see a bit of Liberia, Ghana, Nigeria, and the Congo; to visit South Africa, including the city of Jo-Burg. I had traveled some 300 miles of countryside by minibus on my way to Kruger Park, which gave me a chance to see a lot of the area. I saw the spectacular Victoria Falls from both Rhodesia and Zambia, even from the air by a small private plane. I went for a boat ride up the famous Zambesi River and visited the town of Livingstone. I saw the Nairobi National Park; slept overnight at Treetops; stayed in the Mt. Kenya Safari Club; and visited many of the big game preserves such as the Ngorongoro Crater, Serengeti, Amboseli, and the Masai Mara preserve. I traveled 1,300 miles through Kenya and Tanzania in minibuses and landrovers. I stayed in tents at the edge of the jungle, lulled to sleep by the sounds of animals in the African veldt, and I even slept by Mt. Kilimanjaro. I roomed at the newest and most luxurious hotels in all Africa and saw the continent in both its modern and primitive attire—the big cities, the dense jungles. There was so much to do in three weeks that the first few days in Dakar seemed like years ago, not only to myself but to most of the members of the tour.

This has been a super luxury trip; we have stayed at the finest hotels, eaten the best food, and were treated like royalty. Perhaps the older folks, the seasoned travelers who have been around the world many times, would not be quite as enthusiastic as I was on this, my first, full-length guided tour, for it is all old hat to them. But the younger set, the novice travelers, will have a real treat in store for them. The guided tour is the only way to travel. Previously, I had traveled quite extensively by myself and had to make all my own arrangements. You just can't beat the tour. All your food, lodging, tips, baggage, reservations are handled for you. All you have to do is enjoy yourself. You can't beat that!

The fact that we covered so much ground and saw so many things was because everything had been carefully worked out ahead of time by experts. On a guided tour, all trivial matters are handled by your tour leader. When you arrive in a strange town, he takes your passports and plane tickets and rushes you through customs and immigration with no worries on your part. He checks your luggage for you and sees that it is taken from the plane and transported to your hotel room. He pays all the tips; you don't pay anything unless it is for something special, something you do on your own. For example, we gave our tour leader a tip when we left, and also our guide and driver in Kenya.

We had skilled guides all throughout the trip, men who lived in Africa and who knew the area in which they were working. If we wanted to see elephants they could find them easily, or they would ask someone where they were on that particular day. Elephants walk with such giant steps that they can easily move 50 or 100 miles away from an area in less than a day's time. The only advantage in going it by yourself is that you can stop and go just about as you please, but we still had the opportunity to stop whenever we desired. Also, there is safety in numbers. We traveled in four separate buses. If one bus had broken down in a remote area, the others would have been right there to help.

Another thing that impressed me about the trip was that I saw no hostility of natives toward whites anywhere. I asked an educated Masai if there were any ill feelings between them and he said there were none. In the colonial days there was, but now that the countries are independent, they *want* us to come there, for tourism helps their economy. He said that if a white man's car broke down in the bush, the natives would gladly help him. Of course I would not doubt that there would be an occasional problem in some of the larger cities or perhaps even out in some remote area, but the tour companies, cognizant of this, route their trips accordingly.

I was concerned about having things taken from my room or tent when I was not there, but I was never missing a *single* item from my unlocked suitcases. In fact if you left any small item behind at one place, you would find it in your room at your next location. How it would catch up with you and land in the right room is one of the mysteries of Africa. One time I tried to throw away a number of half-empty toilet articles rather than carry them all the way home. They were promptly removed from the wastebasket and placed

on the cabinet. I finally had to sign a paper stating that I didn't want them so that the natives could keep them. I suspect this is protection against theft. The only thing we were cautioned about leaving in the open was money, which is understandable. One time I left my flashlight in my room. The next day it showed up in my new room 200 miles away! Another time I left my toothbrush behind. There it was waiting for me at the next stop. I lost my sunglasses once. Sure enough, they were returned to me by my guide, John. He said that I had left them on top of the land rover. It's a wonder they hadn't fallen off. I must have put them down to take a picture and forgot about them. I was lucky that time.

My clothing didn't present any problems at all. I found that my one suit, which I wore only a few times in Jo-Burg and in Nairobi, was sufficient. Mostly I wore sport shirts and slacks. My one pair of dress shoes was adequate, and the open-mesh, nylon sneakers that I wore nine tenths of the time were very comfortable. My wash-and-wear shirts and slacks would easily dry out overnight, and I had plenty of time to wash them after dinner. On the actual safari I just took a couple of shirts with me, washing them whenever they needed it. You certainly couldn't wear a suit out in the bush.

I also found that the one dollar bill was good for small purchases all over Africa, just as the travel agent had suggested. If we were to be in an area for several days, our tour leader advised us to purchase $20 worth of local money. It is easier to buy things with local currency as the natives understand its value. Always anticipate your spending needs in each country and spend all your local money before you leave or have it changed back into American dollars at the local bank or at your hotel desk. There usually is a service charge for changing money so you will lose some in the process. Also be sure to send postcards Air Mail and mail them in the country where you buy the stamps. The stamps are no good in the next country. This is important, for on a trip like this you can be in one country one day and another the next. If you forget to mail your cards, you will have to buy new stamps in the next country, and Air Mail is rather expensive.

Traveling all by yourself as I did would not be quite as nice as if you were traveling with your spouse or a good friend. You may be fortunate to travel with a compatible group, or you could end up with a number of chronic complainers who, if you listen to them, could ruin your trip. In our group there were a few who did not share my enthusiasm for the beauty and primitive of wild Africa. I simply pretended that I was by myself and looked out the window at the scenery. This is what I came to Africa for in the first place and I was determined that nothing would ruin my fabulous trip.

I think Steve did a splendid job of catering to the complicated whims of 20 odd people (including myself). The whole trip went exceptionally smooth, almost like clockwork, with no real problems (except for my toothache, which stopped hurting after a week). I did not expect to find a plush hotel, with tuxedo-attired waiters, in the middle of the African bush. I was happy to sleep in tents, especially under the magic spell of Mt. Kilimanjaro. I *enjoyed* being wakened in the early morning by the guide bringing hot tea to my tent or by the singing of a thousand birds. But some people didn't. Many of them said they would never come back to Africa. Me, I would love to come back and I will.

I would strongly recommend that if your main interest is in animals that you take a total animal tour instead of the tour I took. Percival has one called Africa Adventure that goes to Murchison Falls, Queen Elizabeth Park, Nairobi, Masai Mara, Serengeti, Ngorongoro, and Treetops among other places. This is more of a wildlife tour than mine. It would be nice if tours could be arranged for those over 50 and under 50 so that people could be more in their age group. A younger person feels out of place with all old people and visa versa.

I have heard that Murchison Falls is one of the most fabulous wildlife areas of all. It is included in the African Adventure tour as mentioned previously but now Percival has added it to the African Highlight tour which will greatly enhance this tour. I wish I had seen it on my trip. If I had to do it all over again, I think I would *still* have taken the African Highlight tour for it covers the whole African continent while the other tours only go to East Africa, especially since they have added Murchison Falls to it. But I would like to spend *more* time in the wild and *less* in the cities. You see so much in three weeks that it is almost incomprehensible.

We had a very fine dinner, one of the best I have eaten on any plane. Then later in the day we had another lunch with hot coffee. Before I knew it we flew over Boston, then arrived in New York. According to my watch it was 8:45 P.M., but we were informed over the loudspeaker that it was 3:45 P.M. because of the time difference. A few minutes after a smooth landing we were at the terminal. We were told that they had a new, fast customs system in New York instead of the old stop-and-search method.

Once inside the terminal, I stopped at immigration. The man asked for my passport and a form we had filled out on the plane. Then he asked me which countries I had visited and how much I purchased. I told him less than a hundred dollars. He looked into my flight bag briefly, then stamped the passport. Next stop was public health, where they checked the health card, asked which countries I had visited, then stuck a yellow card inside the passport, telling me to give it to a doctor if I got sick within two weeks and to have him notify their department.

Next, I picked up my luggage and walked through customs. No one looked at any of my belongings. I asked one of the men if they were going to check it and he said not unless I wanted them to. I was through customs in one minute. They apparently spot check certain individuals or else they can tell if you are trying to smuggle something. After that, I had to take a bus from the Pan American terminal to the Eastern terminal. This is quite a task when burdened with two suitcases, cameras, and a heavy shoulder bag. I honestly don't know how the women could possibly do it, for they all had bags as heavy or heavier than my own. With all the modern technology, I don't see why there aren't slow-moving conveyor belts in every corridor and passageway in the terminal. Even if you were only carrying a hand bag it would be helpful to put it on a motor driven belt and walk along with it. It is extremely tiring otherwise and there is often a half mile walk to get from the plane door up into the terminal itself.

Finally I made it over to Eastern with all my luggage. I said goodbye to a few of the tour members who were still with me and checked in at the ticket counter. I was worried about being charged for overweight (there is a 44-pound limit), as my luggage now weighed 68 pounds, but the clerk didn't charge me. I was booked on a 5:00 P.M. flight to Miami instead of the 6:30 flight on my reservation, as there was plenty of room on the earlier flight. In 15 minutes we were airborne.

All my original apprehension about making the big trip had vanished long ago. There was really nothing to it! We flew on good planes, mostly jets, and traveled on land in good vehicles with skilled drivers. It was perfectly safe all the way through. Before I was even home, I was already planning another trip to Africa to see other areas like the Mountains of the Moon, Murchison Falls, and the Congo. But that's another book and another great adventure.

The flight to Miami was fast and smooth. The stewardess served champagne (all you wanted) and dinner, but I just couldn't eat, after having about four dinners already the same day. I was absolutely exhausted, ready to fall asleep at any moment. It was hard to believe that I had been all the way to Africa, been on a real safari, and crossed the Atlantic ocean twice—all in three weeks. It seemed like only minutes and we were already approaching Miami. After traveling half way around the world, a flight from Miami to New York is like going to the corner drug store. We landed in Miami at about 7:30 P.M. and I gingerly stepped off the plane. I had made it at last. From start to finish, my trip had gone almost like clockwork. Now I was back in the Miami terminal where my journey had begun.

I went down to claim my luggage. I watched the spiral luggage rack as first one, then the other suitcase came sliding down the ramp. I decided to take a taxi home rather than have my family pick me up as it would be less complicated. As I drove home, I noted changes in the expressway. They were building safety barriers in the median strip. A lot can happen in three weeks. I wondered how things would be at home. Then, before I knew it, we were in front of my house.

As I stopped at the gate, the front door of the house opened and my daughter Julie came running down to the cab, a huge smile on her face. My son Paul followed behind and my wife waited at the door. I was home from Africa!

Then came questions and answers and a two-hour summary of my trip, during which time the suitcases were opened and various gifts presented. My son got his Masai spear, my daughter her African doll and necklaces, my wife her gold earrings and zebra compact. The rest of the items were set aside for later distribution. I was too exhausted to sort them out.

As I dropped off to sleep that night, I began to wonder if it had all been a dream. Had I really been to Africa? Did I really sleep in a tent beside Mt. Kilimanjaro? Then I heard two animals growling outside. I rushed to the window, still thinking I was in a tent in the wilds. It was only our dog growling at the neighbor's dog. Africa was still with me. It had been a fantastic voyage but the adventurer was home at last.

10. Special Photo Hints

If you are going all the way to Africa on a safari you should bring back a great many *good* photos of the animals, the natives, and the scenery. Cameras have been greatly simplified today, but you just cannot get really good pictures with an inexpensive, fixed-focus one. Purchase a camera with a decent quality lens and practice shooting pictures with it long before your trip. Buy it at a regular camera store. It may cost you a little more but the salesman will be able to tell you *how* to use it, which will more than make up for the difference in cost. Today you can buy high-quality cameras with exposure meters built right inside so you don't have to learn how to use the meter at all. You simply aim the camera at your subject and turn a knob until a little circle inside the viewfinder lines up with the needle from the meter. That's all there is to it. You press the shutter and your picture is perfectly exposed every time. It is easy to take professional pictures, but you must have a good camera. Box cameras or fixed-focus cameras (cameras where you don't have

to set the footage) just cannot give you high-quality pictures except at close range.

If you do purchase a high quality camera with a built in exposure meter, then use just one type of film only, like High Speed Ecktachrome or Kodachrome II. If you stick with one kind you won't have to make any changes on the camera for film speed. This is important, for every time you change to a different type of film, you must change the film speed setting or your pictures will not be properly exposed. Professional photographers do this all the time and it is no problem for them because they are accustomed to it. But if you are a beginner, you could easily forget and ruin roll after roll of film. This is why it is best to stick to one type if you are just starting out with new and rather complicated equipment. Learn how to load the camera properly and purchase 36-exposure rolls rather than 20-exposure. This will eliminate constant changing of film.

If you want to get *good,* high-quality pictures, get

a good camera and learn how to use it. Buy a small book on basic photography or join a local camera club and learn the very basic principles of photography, such as *not* shooting into the light, holding the camera steady when you push the shutter, focusing before each shot, etc. A few lessons at a photo club is time and money well spent. Your camera salesman also should instruct you on how to take good pictures. But don't buy your camera from a cut-rate place and then bring it to a camera shop to learn how to operate it. This is unfair.

By all means, *buy a Super 8 movie camera* or even a sound camera, if you are going to Africa. The new models are absurdly simple to operate. I bought a Bell and Howell Super 8 that was so easy to use my ten-year-old son took movies the first day we got it. It is battery-operated so you don't even have to wind it. It also has an electric eye exposure meter so you don't have to set the lens. All you have to do is set the distance or footage, which only takes a second. They even have a focus meter for that. You can eliminate the focusing 99 percent of the time by simply leaving the focus set at infinity, which means that anything and everything beyond 30 feet will be in sharp focus. Practically all of your scenes and shots are farther away than this, so all you will have to do is aim and shoot. For anything closer you can set the footage for a sharp picture, but then swing it back to infinity in case you forget to change it during an exciting shot. Home movies from Africa are great and you will love them.

They will bring the whole trip right back to you in full color. Hold the camera steady when you are taking movies. This is the only really important thing to remember. Also make certain that you shoot enough of each scene so that it will last long enough on the screen to enjoy it. I usually count to about eight for an average scene. Of course if it's an exciting scene of elephants or lions fighting or running, just keep shooting steadily until the action stops or until you run out of film. Again, your dealer will advise you. You can get a good movie camera, film projector, and screen for about $200. That's what the Bell and Howell outfit I used cost me and it worked perfectly. I saw several people with much more expensive movie cameras, who had constant trouble.

Carry an extra set of batteries with you, also take about 25 to 30 rolls of film. This will just about do you for the trip that I took. For still cameras, about 25 or 30 rolls will do fine if you are using 35mm, which is what most people use these days.

If you are really intent on getting a lot of good pictures, don't put all your trust in one still camera—bring two. Remember, one slight bump or drop of your camera, or any kind of mechanical trouble, and you are out of business. We had one lady in our group whose camera fell apart right in the middle of the safari. Her picture taking came to a complete stop. I finally let her take one of my cameras.

I am a photographer by profession so I brought two high-quality still cameras and one Super 8 movie camera. The latter is not a real professional camera but it was fine for my purpose. I just didn't have the room to carry a heavy 16mm movie camera with all my other gear. Also 16mm film is so expensive when compared to super 8. Some professionals are still using it as it is needed in filling their specific needs but many are now switching to Super 8 as it is so much less expensive. My movies came out beautifully. They looked just about as good as those I shot with my 16mm camera in the past.

Special Tips for Better Pictures

When photographing animals, particularly when taking movies, ask your driver *not* to move the vehicle until you have finished. If he drives on just as you are finishing a shot, the end of the scene will be jumpy. Multiply this by several dozen shots and you will have jumpy scenes after *every* shot. Skilled safari drivers will ask if everyone is finished taking pictures before they move on.

Also, request other people in your minibus to sit very still while you are taking a movie. If they move around while you are exposing your film it will show up in the finished movie. You should, of course, do the same for them. A good scene can be ruined by someone moving around in the bus, especially if you are using a telephoto lens.

Never shoot pictures through the glass windows of the bus unless absolutely necessary. Even though the windows are clean, you will usually pick up reflections from inside that will show up and detract from your pictures.

Choose a seat by the window of a plane if you can. This way you can get extra shots of jungle scenery, beautiful cloud formations, and sunrise and sunset—all very beautiful from a plane.

Take movies of signs, particularly those at the entrances to the game preserves. They will add authenticity to your movies and at the same time identify the location of the films. Your driver will be happy to stop while you photograph them.

Keep your camera in a plastic bag or tightly sealed in the case, except when actually taking pictures. Also keep the lens cap on except when shooting. Game preserves and parks are usually extremely dusty and the dust can ruin your camera. Also, carry a small packet of lens tissue in your pocket and wipe off your lens *at least* two or three times a day. A coating of dust on the lens will lessen the crisp quality of your pictures.

Keep both camera and film out of the hot sun at all times. Always put them in the shade. Tropical heat can ruin film quickly. I carried my cameras with me most of the time while on Safari, not even leaving them in the bus. I carried all of my exposed film, movie camera, and several extra rolls of film for the day's shooting in my Percival hand bag, which I slung over my shoulder. My two still cameras were also carried by shoulder strap. I would carry them this way to lunch, so that I would have them with me. In the minibus, you can set them on the seat beside you. I had all my film processed by Kodak when I returned to Miami. This way I feel I get the best work rather than have it mailed from overseas. In some countries it may take several weeks for your film to get back to the states for processing. This could lessen the quality of the finished product.

For Professionals or Advanced Amateurs

I used two still cameras for my safari, bringing the extra camera along for special shots and the added protection of having two cameras. One camera was a Minolta single-lens reflex, with through-the-lens focusing and built-in exposure meter, the latest model. It is superb and very easy to use. I used a 100mm lens on it most of the time and found that it brought the animals up to just the right range. I shot most everything at 250th of a second when possible, dropping down to slower speeds when necessary. This is a very quick focus camera and you can easily get off several shots of a slow moving subject with no special effort.

I used about half, Hi-Speed Ektachrome and Kodachrome II. You may prefer Kodachrome X for some shots.

My other camera was the Alpha with a 40mm wide-angle lens that focuses from infinity all the way down to two inches! This is a superb camera and I used it for scenic shots where I wanted to take in a vast area. Also I used it for closeup shots where I wanted to get very close to the subject.

I found that the two cameras gave me practically all of the coverage I needed. I had a 300mm telephoto lens with me but found little opportunity to use it as there was far too much movement in the minibus. Also there was not enough time to set up the camera with the long lens. In fact, the only place I could use it at all was at Treetops or at the rest camps. But it was useful there. I would *still recommend* bringing a long lens and a tripod or unipod if possible. In areas such as Murchison Falls, Tsavo, and many of the other parks, you can set up the camera from your lodge and get fabulous bird photos or game shots. Bird photographers in particular will positively need a long lens. Most of the regular game can easily be photographed with a four- or six-inch lens. Sometimes even these are too long.

I registered my cameras with customs in New York before leaving the country and stuck the slip in my pocket. It only took a few minutes. The cameras were not checked when I came back into the country, but if they had been this would have saved a lot of time. I found no special photo problems taking pictures in Africa. I brought nearly all of my film with me rather than purchase it abroad, and put each roll back into its can or box after exposing it. I had no trouble with heat or moisture. Most of my film came out well, simply by following standard photographic technique.

11.   List of Game Preserves and National Parks

KENYA

Nairobi National Park—44 square miles. Just four miles from downtown. Contains lions, giraffe, zebra, everything except elephant.

Tsavo National Park—8,034 square miles. Stronghold for elephants, over 20,000 in the area. One of the largest animal preserves in Africa.

Amboseli Game Reserve—1,259 square miles. Magnificent view of Mt. Kilimanjaro; elephant, rhino, beautiful tenting area.

Marsabit Mountain Reserve—806 square miles. Features game seldom seen elsewhere; northern Kenya; a remote park, special permission required.

Samburu Game Reserve—60 square miles. Grevy Zebra, reticulated giraffe, other unusual species; northern Kenya.

Buffalo Springs Game Reserve—80 square miles. Greater kudu, desert birds, rhino, and buffalo; northern Kenya.

Meru Game Reserve—Located northeast of Mt. Kenya. Offers fishing and even bird shooting.

Masai-Mara Reserve—700 square miles. Adjoins Serengeti; very wild; armed guards ride with you; elephant, lions, buffalo in great numbers.

Lake Nakuru—18 square miles. Largest concentration of flamingos in the world, sometimes two million inhabit the lake; also 300 species of other birds; approximately 100 miles from Nairobi.

Aberdare National Park—228 square miles. Forest animals, elephant, buffalo, famous Treetops Hotel; dense rain forests, interesting vegetation, particularly on the higher slopes.

Mt. Kenya National Park—Interesting forest area; bongo and other antelope rarely seen elsewhere; famous Secret Valley Lodge; dense rain forests; leopards nearly always can be seen at the lodge, making it unique.

Mt. Elgon National Park—Dense forests, bongo, rare antelope; one of Kenya's newest parks.

Shimba Hills Game Reserve—Just 30 miles from Mombassa; home of the sable antelope, as well as other species.

For additional information about Kenya write: Ministry of Information, P. O. Box 30025, Nairobi, Kenya, Africa.

TANZANIA

Serengeti National Park—5,000 square miles. Stretches westward almost to Lake Victoria. Some of the largest concentrations of animals in the world; it has a quarter million gazelle, 350,000 wildebeeste, 20,000 buffalo, and 19,000 giraffe just to mention a few; beautiful lodge and tents; a fabulous place.

Arusha National Park—45 square miles. Includes Momela Lakes, Ngurdoto Crater, and other interesting areas; many birds as well as wildlife; many rhino here; attractive game lodge.

Lake Manyara National Park—123 square miles. A famous widlife area where the lions stay in trees; also has elephant, rhino, many birds, beautiful scenery; you can watch game from your lodge.

Ruaha National Park—5,000 square miles. Has an abundance of wildlife including roan and sable antelope, as well as many other species.

Mikumi National Park—450 square miles. Elephant, giraffe, zebra, and lion, as well as most of the other species.

Ngorongoro Conservation Area—3,200 square miles. One of the most interesting areas. The crater is 102 square miles in area and is filled with animals; rhino, hyena, lion, wildebeest, zebra, and elephant live here, just to mention a few; fine lodge at crater rim.

Mikumi National Park—450 square miles. Park abounds in zebra, elephant, giraffe, and other species.

For additional information on Tanzania write: Tanganyika National Tourist Board, P. O. Box 2485, Dar es Salaam, Tanzania, Africa.

UGANDA

Queen Elizabeth National Park—800 square miles. Many hippo, elephant, buffalo, kob, giant forest hogs, and chimpanzee, as well as other species; a rich, green, lake-studded area with enormous wildlife herds.

Murchison Falls National Park—1,504 square miles. Huge Nile river passes through tiny rock passage, a spectacle in itself; area teeming with wildlife; famous for its crocodiles, hippo, and elephant.

Kidepo Valley National Park—500 square miles. A new

park in one of the wildest parts of Uganda; greater and lesser kudu, roan antelope, and many less common species.

For additional information on Uganda write: Uganda Tourist Association, P. O. Box 1542, Kampala, Uganda, Africa.

THE CONGO

Albert National Park—3,124 square miles. Mountains of the moon, elephant, gorillas, chimpanzee, strange plants, rain forests, okapi and other unusual dwellers of the forest.
Upemba National Park—4,528 square miles. Extremely wild area; elephant, buffalo, and all the rest.
Garamba National Park—1,900 square miles. A wild, untouched area with big game of all kinds.
Kagera National Park—970 square miles. Variety of all kinds of animals both large and small.
Note: See your travel agency for details in accommodations and information to the various parts in Africa.

SENEGAL

Niokolo Koba National Park—1,900 square miles. Elephant, buffalo, hippo, many kinds of birds, antelope, as well as monkeys of all kinds.
For brochure write: Socopao Voyages, 3 Place De L'Independance, Dakar, Senegal, Africa.

SOUTH AFRICA

Kruger National Park—7,340 square miles. One of the most famous national parks: dense brush, elephant, zebra, lions, and both black as well as white rhino.
Write: The Director, Kruger National Park, Skukuza, South Africa
Umfolozi and Hluhuwe Game Reserves—120,000 acres. Over 1,000 white rhino live in this small area; world's stronghold for the species; also has black rhino, nyala, kudu, and lesser game; foot safaris are common with guide.
Write: Umfolozi Game Preserve, Box 99, Mtubatuba, Natal, Sululand, S.A.
Bontebok National Park—5½ square miles. Bontebok, hartebeest, grysbok, and other game.
Kalahari National Park—3,650 square miles. Herds of thousands of gemsbok, springbok, hartebeest, lions, ostrich; largely desert.
Gemsbok National Park—4,300 square miles. Similar to Kalahari.

Addo Elephant Park—26 square miles. Extremely dense bush; home of the famous Addo elephants that shun humans; 50 elephants, antelope, lesser game, birds of all kinds, reptiles.
Mountain Zebra National Park—17 square miles. Exclusive park for protection of mountain zebra, which are extremely rare; also contains various antelope and lesser game.
Write: The Director, National Parks Board, Andries and Pretorius Street, Pretoria, South Africa

RHODESIA

Wankie National Park—5,000 square miles. Over 7,000 elephant, huge buffalo herds, both black and white rhino, all kinds of game.
Rhodes Matopos National Park—1,200 square miles. Just South of Bulawayo; huge boulders, hidden valleys, all kinds of game; both black and white rhinos, klipspringer, and all the rest.
Kyle Game Reserve—Oribi, giraffe, white rhino, all the rest; located alongside Lake Kyle.
For further information on Rhodesia's parks, write: Secretary, Wildlife Society of Rhodesia, P.O. Box 3497, Salisbury, Rhodesia.

ZAMBIA

Kafue National Park—8,650 square miles. Elephant, buffalo, red leche, all the rest; said to be Africa's largest national park.
Luanga Valley National Park—6,000 square miles. A wild, untouched wilderness; over 20,000 elephant, buffalo, rare thornicroft giraffe, kudu; game safaris on foot with armed guard.

For further information write: The Zambia National Tourist Bureau, P.O. Box 17, Lusaka, Zambia, Africa.

Note: The above is only a partial list of Africa's game parks and preserves. There are many more, and additional ones are being created each year. You will note that the parks vary in size. This does not mean that the smaller parks are not worth visiting. Some of them contain unique species found only in their area. Many of the parks publish pamphlets or small books with great detail about themselves. For countries not listed above, simply write to the Tourist Bureau in the capitol of the country in which you are interested. Please mention the author's book.

Suggested Reading

The following books and periodicals will provide additional information on Africa, particularly its parks and wildlife.

Africa, A Natural History, by Leslie Brown, Random House. A very large, fabulous book on Africa and all its animals. Price: $20.

Nature's Paradise, by Des Bartlett, Collins. A large book on Africa's animals, with superb photos. Price: $20.

Great National Parks of the World, by Richard Carrington, Random House, $20.00. Gives detail of the world's parks. Large and beautifully illustrated.

Animals of East Africa, by C. A. Spinage, Houghton Mifflin, $7.50.

Rhinos Belong to Everyone, by Dr. Grzimek. A beautiful, large book.

Serengeti Shall Not Die, by Bernhard and Michael Grzimek, Hamish Hamilton.

Field Guide to Birds of East and Central Africa, by John G. Williams, Collins.

Field Guide to the National Parks of East Africa, by John G. Williams, Collins.

Born Free, Living Free, Forever Free, all by Joy Adamson, Harcourt, Brace & World, $5.95.

Pamphlets, with approximate price

Exploring East Africa, by East Africa Travel Association, free

Kenya and National Parks of Uganda and Tanzania, 5/- $2.00 or $3.00 air mail. Write: Editorial Service, Karen Rd., P.O. Box 24886, Nairobi, Kenya

Serengeti National Park, $1.00

Zambia Travel Guide, Free. Zambia National Tourist Bureau, Box 17, Lusaka, Zambia

Animals of Rhodesia, 50¢

Birds of Rhodesia, 50¢

Rhodesia Calls, 50¢

Safari Magazine, P.O. Box 30339, Nairobi, Kenya, 50¢ copy

Africana, quarterly animal magazine, $5.00 yr. East African Wildlife Society, P.O. Box 20110, Nairobi, Kenya

Animals, monthly, 21 Great Castle Street, London W1N 8LT, England, $9.00 yr.

Congo Kitabu by Jean-Pierre Hallet, Random House, $6.95

Guide to Kruger National Park $1.50

Percival Tours Brochure, 5820 Wilshire Blvd., Los Angeles, Calif. 90036, free

Pan American World Airways Route Map Booklet, 200 Park Ave., New York, N.Y., free

New Horizons World Guide, 832 pages with facts about 138 countries, by Gerald W. Whitted. This is a fabulous book with detailed information on many countries, including Africa, $3.00 from Pan Am Publications, P.O. Box 757, Melville, N.Y. 11746

Safari, 320 pages, is a Pan Am guide to safaris in 77 countries, $5.95 from Pan Am Publications, P.O. Box 757, Melville, N.Y. 11746

Shell Maps of Kenya and Tanzania. These are large, full color maps of Kenya on waterproof paper. You can derive much pleasure from them and plot out your route in advance. One map covers Kenya, Uganda and Tanzania. $2.00 Write: Shell Drivers Club, Box 3561, Nairobi, Kenya, Africa (Shell booklets also available)

Index